Equine Nutrition

Derek Cuddeford

The Crowood Press

First published in 1996 by
The Crowood Press Ltd
Ramsbury, Marlborough
Wiltshire SN8 2HR

www.crowood.com

Paperback edition 2003

British Library Cataloguing-in-Publication Data
A catalogue record for this book is available from the British Library.

ISBN 1 86126 565 4

Photographs by Robert Munro

Line-drawings by Elizabeth Mallard-Shaw, except those on pages 26,
35–6, 49, 50, 58, 63, 67 (bottom), 77, 101, 115, 128, 149, 152, which
are by Rhona Muirhead.

Acknowledgements
Special thanks are due to Vanessa Britton for her help in producing
the manuscript.

Figs 12, 13 and 14 adapted from L.B. Jeff Cott, *et al.*, *Equine
Veterinary Journal*, **18**:97–101 (1986); Figs 17 and 18 from G.H.
Waring, *Horse Behaviour*, Noyes Publications, New Jersey, USA
(1983); Table 9.1 sourced from NRC, *Nutrient Requirements of Horses*
(5th rev. edn), National Academy Press, Washington DC (1989); Table
10.2 and Fig 26 adapted from *The Horse in Winter: Shelter and
Feeding*, the Scottish Agricultural College, Aberdeen (1991).

Typeset and designed by D & N Publishing,
Lambourn Woodlands, Hungerford, Berkshire

Printed and bound in Great Britain by Bookcraft (Bath) Ltd

CONTENTS

1 Evolution   5

2 Early Horse Behaviour   14

3 Digestion   19

4 Nutrients and their Absorption   29

5 Minerals   40

6 Vitamins   48

7 Grassland   57

8 Conventional Feeds   74

9 Compound Feeds   90

10 Feeding for Maintenance   98

11 Feeding for Breeding and Growth   109

12 Feeding for Performance   121

13 Clinical Nutrition and Food-Related Problems   133

14 Ration Formulation   148

Index   159

To my young 'nags',
Morag, Harriet and Emily

1
EVOLUTION

Modern-day horse still displays many of the characteristics that his ancient ancestors possessed millions of years ago. While today's horse is largely a domesticated animal, he is still born with the natural instincts of his predecessors, who had to defend themselves against predators and survive despite a constantly changing world. Thus, the evolution of the horse has a significant bearing on the way in which we should keep and feed him in current times. In order to satisfy the basic needs of the horse and to recognize what his 'natural' behaviour is, it helps to have an understanding of how and why he evolved as he did.

The first predecessor of modern-day horse appeared on the earth some 55 million years ago, during what was known as the Eocene period. He was a rabbit-like animal called *Eohippus*, or 'the Dawn Horse', which had four toes, a stumpy neck, and eyes which were set to the front of his head (*see* Fig 1). His diet consisted mainly of shrubs which grew within the swampy, forested areas in which he lived.

Successive equine generations went through marked changes until the horse became as we know him today. The most significant of these changes included:

1. An increase in size, which changed remarkably from that of a rabbit, through to that of a sheep and then an ass, until he reached the size of the modern-day horse. This adaptation allowed more room for a larger heart and lungs, necessary for when the horse had to flee quickly from predators. It also provided space for the development of a complicated digestive system, necessary to process the cellulose-rich vegetation of his new environment.

2. An increase in speed, due to a lengthening and strengthening of the limb bones, which meant that provided the horse reacted quickly enough he would be able to make a hasty retreat when necessary.

3. A lengthening of the head and neck to enable him to graze at floor level, together with modifications of the skull, so that the eyes were positioned at the sides of the head to facilitate all-round vision.

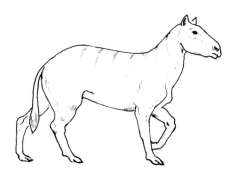

Fig 1 Eohippus, *also known as* Hyracotherium *or the Dawn Horse, was about the size of a fox.* Eohippus *lived about 55 million years ago, evolving gradually into* Mesohippus, *who appeared about 35 million years ago.*

Environmental Effects

The predecessors of modern-day horse saw significant climatic changes, and these dictated their evolution. As tropical vegetation gave way to extensive grasslands, their body design responded accordingly, enabling them to live in unforested areas.

At the same time, taller, swifter and more intelligent carnivores were evolving, which became the natural predators of the horse. In response the horse developed a digestive system which could cope with the mastication and processing of large quantities of grass, and a flight reflex which enabled him to run swiftly and

Fig 2 Merychippus, *who appeared about 25 million years ago.*

accurately from enemies, to which he was now clearly visible. Thus the horse developed into a successful herbivore, capable of defending himself by fleeing from any life-threatening situation.

It starts to become clear then, why, given access to both a warm and comfortable stable with a net full of hay or a paddock with sufficient grazing, modern horses will choose to live out of doors whatever the weather. The desire for comfort and warmth is a human trait that has no part in the horse's natural way of life. Similarly their natural instincts will direct them to run from any frightening situation rather than to stand up and fight; another reason why they prefer the freedom of an open field. Shut them in stables and you prevent them from being able to act upon their natural instincts.

DIGESTIVE DEVELOPMENT

Examination of the teeth taken from fossil remains suggests that the precursors of today's horse deliberately selected high-fibre diets such as the stems and leaves of plants, rather than the berries, seeds and fruits. This posed a nutritional problem for the horse, as such fibrous material contains large amounts of a polysaccharide cellulose within its cell walls.

Problems arose because the horse did not produce any enzyme which was successful at breaking down this cellulose; and he was therefore deprived of both its nutritional value and that of the cell contents it surrounds. In order to combat this problem the horse developed in two ways.

Firstly, a mutually beneficial relationship was formed with organisms capable of breaking down cellulose. Secondly, the horse's caecum (a part of the digestive tract, *see* Fig 3), and colon expanded in order to a provide a site where the breakdown process, known as fermentation, could take place. This is known as hind-gut fermentation. Interestingly, ruminants (as represented by the modern-day cow or sheep) of the same period, enlarged their stomachs in order to overcome the problem *(see* Fig 4), a digestive process known as fore-gut fermentation.

THE FERMENTATION PROCESS

The actual process of fermentation appears to be identical in both horses and ruminants, but surprisingly horses digest cellulose-rich vegetation with only 70 per cent of the efficiency of ruminants. This is related to the differences in size of the digestive tract for each animal type. The digestive tract of a horse and its contents comprise about 15 per cent of his bodyweight, and the time it takes for food to pass through this tract is on average about forty-eight hours. By comparison, the cow's digestive tract and contents comprise about 40 per cent of its bodyweight, where food can take anything from seventy to ninety hours to pass through. The reason for this is that the cow, unlike the horse, has a restricting orifice between parts of its gut which only allows small particles to pass through; therefore it has an extended fermentation time and has to

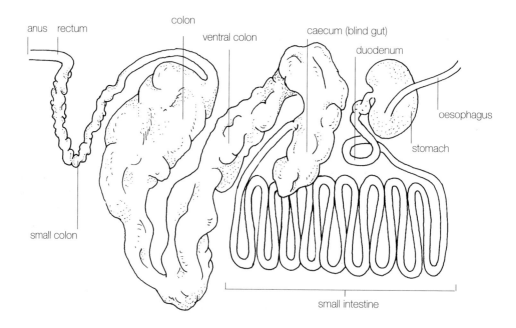

Fig 3 *The digestive system of the horse.*

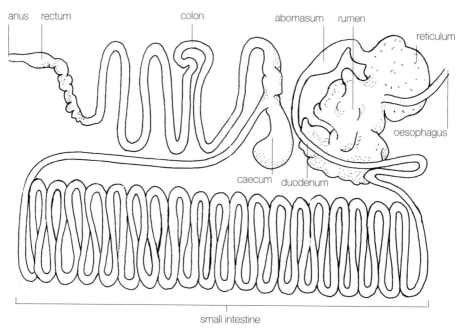

Fig 4 *The digestive system of the ruminant.*

'chew the cud' (regurgitate its food and chew it again) in order to reduce particle size.

Assuming that there is an adequate feed supply, the horse's digestive system would enable him to survive on a fibrous diet upon which cows of a similar body size could not. This is purely due to the horse's greater intake, even taking into account that this is at the expense of efficient cellulose digestion.

Utilization of Feed Resources

Although horses and cattle are both herbivores and can share the same environment, their different evolutionary paths have had profound effects on the way in which they use their feed resources. For example, in the horse there is no absorptive area after the fermentation site, similar to the small intestine of the cow, and this leads to a loss of various nutrients in the dung. However, this is partly offset by the fact that valuable nutrients such as starch and glucose may be effectively digested. Subsequently these nutrients are absorbed, and not, as in the cow, fermented randomly and often wastefully.

An example of the difference this makes is seen when glucose is fed to both the horse and cow. In the horse a rise in plasma values is observed, but no such rise is seen in the cow. Similarly, providing vegetable oil to ruminants can have disastrous effects on their digestion because it upsets the fermentation system, whereas in horses it is extremely well tolerated.

Specialized Features of the Horse

We have seen that the first adaptation required for the evolving horse so that he could use grass as a food, was the ability to digest it by means of caecal fermentation. However, while the horse could effectively deal with such fibrous foods once ingested, he also needed an efficient system of processing them before they were swallowed. Therefore, the next adaptation was the development of teeth that could effectively cut and chew grass.

Molar Teeth

The consequence of chewing large amounts of grass is considerable tooth wear, due to the abrasive substance called silica which grass contains. This sand-like substance gradually wears away the teeth, and in a natural environment, the life-span of the horse would be limited by the length of time that his teeth remained effective and functional. Nowadays it is possible to keep geriatric, toothless horses alive by feeding mashes, coarse mixes and pre-ground roughages soaked to form a slurry that can be 'slurped up' (*see* Chapter 13).

In order to cope with the demands of his 'rough' diet, during the process of evolution the horse's teeth became more durable. There were a number of structural features that contributed towards this increased durability, and today's grazing animals may possess one or more of the following:
1. An increase in the number of cusps (raised points on the surface of the tooth).
2. An interconnection of these cusps, which

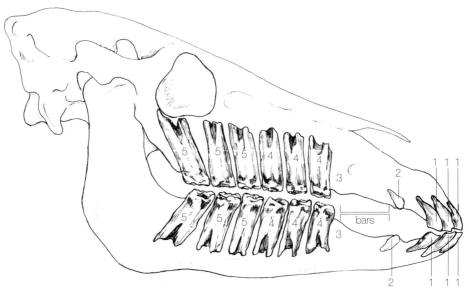

1 Incisors (nippers): total 12
2 Canines (tushes): total 4. (Absent or rudimentary in the mare.)
3 Site of the wolf teeth when present: possible total 4.
4 Premolars: total 12.
5 Molars: total 12.

Fig 5 Dental features of a modern horse.

produces a complex pattern of exposed enamel on the crown of the tooth.

3. An alternation of bands of material of different degrees of hardness on the crown, resulting in differential wear and consequently self-sharpening edges.

4. An increase in the overall size of individual grinding teeth.

5. The development of high crowned teeth that are tall from root to crown.

6. The formation of grinding teeth into a uniform series which provides a composite grinding surface.

In order to accommodate these changes in tooth structure, the skull shape had to change. As the teeth became longer, the upper and lower jaws became deeper which produced the characteristic 'wedge-shape' skull of the modern horse. As the battery of high-crowned grinding teeth lengthened, so did the upper and lower jaws. This resulted in a forward movement of the upper platform, which prevented the roots of the most posterior molars from interfering with the eye orbit (*see* Fig 6).

Skull

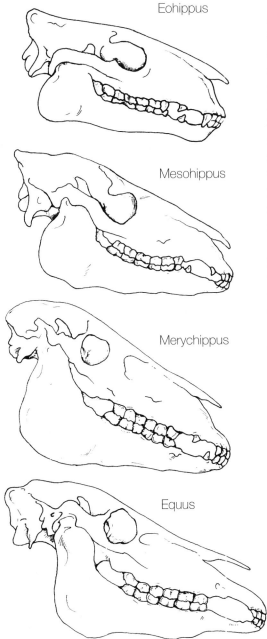

Eohippus

Mesohippus

Merychippus

Equus

Another adaptation which took place during the evolution of the horse was a compression of the ear region and a restriction upon jaw articulation. The result of this was that backwards and forwards movement of the jaw became very limited, which resulted in the characteristic 'side-to-side' chewing movement that we observe in the horse today. The nasal bones extended as far forward as the first incisors, and instead of the lower jawbones meeting in a 'V' they formed a broad, spoon-shaped region in which the lower incisors were bedded. The front part of the lower jaw bent upwards so that the upper and lower incisors met together to form 'nippers', which were (and still are) crucial to the effective harvesting of food. The areas for attaching muscle at the back of the jaw were large, indicating the importance of the chewing mechanism in breaking down fibrous foods.

A reduction in the length of the nasal bones was also achieved, which gave way to the presence of a flexible upper lip and highly mobile nostrils, all of which are used in the selection and grasping of food.

Fig 6 Evolutionary development of the skull from Eohippus *to* Equus.

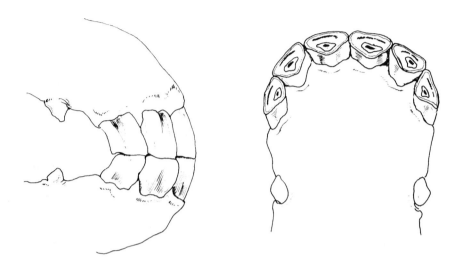

Fig 7 The front jaw shape of the modern horse. The incisors of the upper and lower jaws meet together to form 'nippers'.

Incisor Teeth

It has been suggested that the shape of the muzzle of hoofed animals may be related to differences in diet. However, while most modern horses are kept in controlled environments (field or stable) and are offered fairly uniform diets, we still see differences in their eating behaviour and in the pattern or curvature of horses' and ponies' incisors. This might not greatly affect the confined animal that is well supplied with food, but it could contribute to the 'survivability' of the native pony.

Grazers and browsers have distinct differences in mouth shape, especially in the curvature of the incisor teeth. While a horse will browse, the material collected will only form a small part of his diet. The reduced curvature of the horse's incisor teeth presents a flatter cutting surface to the food plants or grassland which comprise his diet, and enhances his ability to harvest this sort of food. Conversely, the increased curvature of a browser's incisor teeth reduces the cutting surface and so enhances his ability to be selective in what he eats. Thus, while the horse may be less selective in what he eats, he will be able to maximize the rate of food intake. The benefit of this is seen when forage is in short supply, such as in winter-time.

Observation of Exmoor ponies in the UK grazing short grasslands shows that they have a rapid biting rate and, clearly, the effectiveness of each bite will be enhanced if the pony has minimal incisor curvature; indeed, a narrow pointed shape would greatly reduce the ponies' ability to survive.

Summary Points

- Even when *Eohippus* enjoyed a tropical forest environment he deliberately selected a high-fibre diet, such as plant stems and leaves.
- The shift towards a cooler, drier environment resulted in seasonal growth patterns and more fibrous food materials, which forced a need for a fermentation process in the digestive system.
- Caecal/colonic fermentation developed, in contrast to ruminants of the same period which developed a fore-stomach site of fermentation.
- Modern-day horse shows the same characteristics as *Eohippus* and thus the provision of a high-fibre diet is basic to a need which has evolved over the millennia.
- Feeding low-fibre diets invites problems and is the root cause of most of the serious metabolic problems seen in horses today.
- Although both the horse and the cow are herbivores, they utilize their food resources in different ways.
- The adaptations which have taken place in the horse's skull and teeth enable him to exert tremendous crushing forces which, in combination with the side to side shearing action of the jaw, effectively reduces fibrous foodstuffs into small particles.
- Within current horse and pony populations there is a diversity of head and mouth shapes, which might not be important to the confined animal, but which may place the native pony at an advantage relative to other horse species when food is scarce.

2

EARLY HORSE BEHAVIOUR

Does horse behaviour depend upon genetic make-up: is it natural for the horse to behave as he does? Or is it the horse's environment which regulates his behaviour: has he been nurtured to behave as he does? Nowadays, horse behaviour is considered to be the result of an interaction between nature and nurture. Some functions are essential to his survival and are therefore strictly mapped out in the genes. Good examples of these are the 'flight' reaction to threat and the reproductive patterns which the horse knows how to perform without ever being taught. There are others directed towards the horse's survival, too, and of particular importance in this respect is feeding behaviour. As we have seen in Chapter 1, this evolved in response to changing feed resources, and changes in the horse's digestive system took place as a result. Therefore, today's domesticated horse has an inborn feeding behaviour which is well developed and highly motivated, and if, by the employment of mod-ern husbandry techniques, we prevent the horse from 'performing' in this way, problems may arise.

NORMAL FEEDING BEHAVIOUR

Free-living horses have a powerful motivation to forage for food over something like a sixteen-hour period each day. Fig 8 summarizes the main activities of horses and shows how important the time spent feeding is, in relation to other activities; it is clear that feeding is the main occupation of feral horses. It is worth noting, too, that the behaviour closest to feeding in terms of duration is resting. This may be achieved in the upright stance and involve slow-wave sleep, or the horse may be lying down. It is only when the horse is lying down that he can enjoy proper paradoxical sleep; rapid eye movement (REM) sleep occurs at this time.

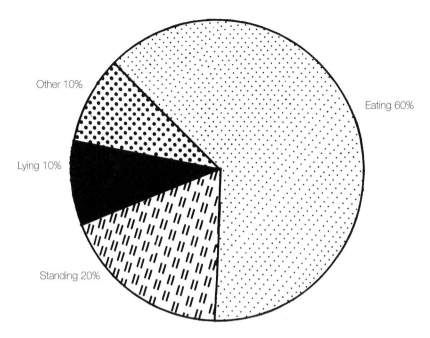

Fig 8 Average occupation of Camargue horses throughout the year.

Interestingly, confining horses in pastures and paddocks does not alter the way in which they allocate their time, even where there is an abundance of herbage. For example, the first line of Table 2.1 shows that the time such horses spend in eating is very similar to that given in Fig 8. However, everything does not always run smoothly for the horse and his patterns of behaviour can be affected by a number of factors:
• Wind and driving rain will force him to seek shelter, thereby interrupting his feeding behaviour.
• Continuous inclement weather can substantially reduce the time spent grazing which, during the winter months, is largely during the day.
• In hot climates the horse may seek shelter during the day and concentrate his feeding activity during the hours of darkness, which limits his intake.
• The presence of biting flies can force horses to stop grazing, perhaps in order to herd together for mutual benefit and so reduce the individual fly burden.

The horse would appear to have a 'maximum' feeding period amounting to some 60 to 70 per cent of his total available time out of each 24-hour period. So even if there is a shortage of available herbage, the horse will not continue to eat for very long over his feeding budget, even though he really needs to do so in order to gain enough food for his needs. Similarly, a horse faced with an abundance of herbage will not reduce his time spent feeding. Thus the horse on sparse grazing will get thinner, and the one with an abundance of food will get fatter, which leads to the conclusion that horses are not nutritionally wise.

While the time spent feeding does not alter much, the way in which the horse feeds may. This is governed by the availability of food at the time of year. For instance, in summer, horses will often browse on shoots or shrubs, bushes and trees, possibly reflecting a more primitive feeding behaviour, but not necessarily because they are hungry. During the autumn and winter, this browsing activity may increase dramatically in relation to the horse's hunger, many horses showing a preference for trees such as beech, poplar, ash and rowan. In areas where grazing is in short supply it is not unusual for bark-eating to become a major problem. It is thought that this may be due to the horse retaining traces of his ancestor's browsing behaviour, although the true reason is not thoroughly understood.

On short grass pastures horses will eat very close to ground level. They are able to do so because they have both upper and lower incisors which meet precisely together. However, on grass pastures which are at least 7cm (3in) high, horses will take a mouthful of grass using their mobile top lip and teeth. One bite of grass will then be followed by a number of chews to crush the grass leaves to a mass that can be swallowed easily. On very short grass, the number of chews per bite is greatly reduced because the amount taken into the mouth following each bite is much smaller. Therefore, there can be a considerable difference in the' bite-to-chew' ratio between long and short grass. Where the horse has to graze on short grass, he will

Feral horses will spend most of their time eating.

Table 2.1 Effect of feed type on time spent in abnormal behaviour in the horse

Environment	No. of horses	Feed	Feed level	% Time spent in feeding	% Time spent in abnormal activities
Pasture	6	grass	A	58	0
Box	5	hay	A	55	2
Tie stall	5	hay	A	64	<1
Tie stall	4	hay	M	60	2
Tie stall	4	pelleted hay	M	10	58
Tie stall	4	alfalfa/ maize cobs	M	12	66

(A = *ad lib*; M = maintenance)

use considerably more energy in gaining the food, than if he had access to longer grass. Furthermore, the close proximity of the soil surface means that the horse is much more likely to ingest soil. This situation can cause excessive tooth wear, a reduction in food utilization, and on sandy soils can lead to bouts of sand colic. However, a horse will only graze poorer areas if he is forced to do so through hunger. Observation of ponies grazing heather moorland interspersed with grassy patches shows that they will avoid the heather – a poorer quality food – until they have exhausted the grassy patches.

Contrary to popular belief, horses will not seek out sources of essential nutrients in which they may be deficient. In addition, they have been shown to be incapable of correcting any mineral deficiency, even when offered a feed which is rich in the mineral that they lack. A tendency or even craving to eat soil is often thought to result from a mineral deficiency, but many non-deficient horses also display such behaviour. Another popular belief is that horses can distinguish between poisonous and harmless plants. This is not the case, however, except perhaps where a plant has a very bitter taste. For instance horses have been shown to become repeatedly ill after eating buttercups, without apparently learning that the plant is harmful.

How Stabling Affects Normal Behaviour

As long as a stabled horse has access to a constant supply of roughage, he will show similar feeding behaviour to that demonstrated by horses at pasture; the time spent in this activity will be almost unaltered (*see* Table 2.1) even if he is severely confined to a stall. However, the time budget for other activities is affected. For example, because he doesn't have the opportunity to socialize, he will spend more time resting, although he may be less willing to rest properly in a confined space, preferring to stand rather than lie down. So, while he may spend at least 60 per cent of available time feeding, which mirrors that of the free-living horse, very little time is spent lying down, which reflects how inhibited the horse feels about doing this in a confined space.

This picture changes considerably when the horse's feeding management is adjusted in order for him to undertake work. The change usually involves the introduction of hard feed (concentrate) and a reduction in roughage (hay), the overall effect being to increase the nutrient density of the diet, in other words to pack the horse's nutrient needs into less bulk. A horse fed in this way will obviously spend less time feeding and so will often try to find other ways of occupying himself: it is when his feeding motivation is frustrated that he is likely to develop abnormal behaviour such as cribbiting and weaving Table 2.1 shows that there appears to be a direct link between the time spent feeding and the performance of this sort of behaviour, and that any restriction on feeding time is likely to lead to vices. To some extent, exercise can be used to occupy the period where the horse would normally continue to feed on roughage, so that his total time budget is filled. In other words, he has no 'time' to develop bad habits – although some horses do not seem to have accepted this theory!

Summary Points

- Today's domesticated horse has a well developed and highly motivated feeding behaviour.
- Problems may arise if we prevent the horse from following his natural feeding pattern.
- Feeding is the main occupation of free-living horses, with resting closest to it in terms of duration.
- Confining horses in pastures and paddocks does not alter the way in which they allocate their time, although their patterns of behaviour can be affected by a number of different factors.
- Horses have a maximum feeding period of about sixteen hours a day.
- Horses are not nutritionally wise.
- Horses cannot distinguish between poisonous and harmless plants.
- When a horse is stabled, provided he has a constant supply of roughage, his time budget for feeding will not alter, although time budgets for other activities will.
- A horse that is not offered a constant supply of roughage will find other ways to fill his time budget for eating.
- If a work-related diet results in the horse having to spend less time eating than he would normally, he is likely to develop vices to occupy his 'spare' feeding time.

3
DIGESTION

FOOD SELECTION

The horse's upper lip is an extremely mobile organ. While being strong, it is also extremely sensitive which helps the horse to sift through the herbage or feed that is on offer. Once appropriate food material has been selected, this top lip will then manoeuvre it into place between the horse's incisors, ready for cutting. Thus the horse can bite off pieces of food material in a very selective fashion and can, if necessary, graze a pasture very closely.

This selection process starts with the upper lip bringing material into the mouth for a closer inspection. While still held by the top lip, the material may be cut by the incisors, only then to be rejected. It may be that cutting of the herbage releases sap and other plant materials which enables a further judgement on the suitability of the material for consumption to be made. This can often be seen by observing a horse for a few minutes in the paddock. Every so often you will see his lips moving in an effort to discard material from his mouth, even though to the human eye it may

appear identical to a previously consumed mouthful. Once cut material is found to be suitable, the horse's tongue will then manoeuvre the food between the molars on each side of the jaw.

The Role of the Teeth

In contrast to the biting action of the incisors, the molars crush and grind through a combination of lateral and vertical movements (*see* Chapter 1). This can result in uneven tooth wear so that in time the inner edges of the lower molars and the outer edges of the upper molars become pointed; these points can cause the horse discomfort by damaging the cheeks and tongue respectively. A horse that is afflicted in this way may be seen dropping partially masticated food from the mouth, a circumstance known as quidding. It is easily rectified, however, by having a qualified person rasp the teeth. Regular inspection is essential, and since the horse depends so much on the successful processing of food within the mouth, this problem should never be allowed to arise.

The grinding of food lasts a considerable time and is accompanied by the production of a lot of saliva, which over a 24-hour period may amount to some 13 litres (approximately 3 gallons). The time spent chewing will be governed by the type of food eaten, whether concentrate or roughage. So, saliva production will also depend on food type, since saliva is only produced when the horse is actually chewing.

Food Processing in the Mouth

Having selected a suitable mouthful, the next stage of digestion is to process the food within the mouth. When food is chewed in the presence of saliva it is moistened, since saliva contains mucus which acts as a lubricant and aids the chewing and physical breakdown of food. The particles become smaller and the addition of the saliva helps to hold them together until they are sufficiently mashed that the horse can swallow the mixture with ease. Saliva also contains bicarbonate which plays an important role in neutralizing excess acid in the first part of the stomach.

Problems can occur with food which needs little chewing as only small amounts of saliva will be produced, resulting in poor acid neutralization. This can be particularly significant with starchy foods which may be fermented quite rapidly and produce acid. Thus a concentrate feed which has been consumed very quickly may suffer an insufficient addition of saliva during mouth processing; the resulting mass may lie for too long in the stomach, and in this

instance will undergo an abnormal fermentation characterized by the production of excessive amounts of gases such as carbon dioxide, hydrogen and methane. This may result in a gas colic of the type frequently suffered by stable-kept horses.

So it is clear that in order to avoid digestive upsets and to ensure well-being, all food materials must be thoroughly and effectively processed in the mouth before swallowing.

The Act of Chewing

In order to compensate for the fact that their teeth are exposed to considerable wear and tear, horses (and ponies) possess molar teeth which constantly erupt through the gum. It is the nature of the food which is fed that governs the number of chewing movements. For example, over 3,000 jaw movements have been recorded in horses consuming 1kg (2½lb) of hay (See Tables 3.1 and 3.2.). Interestingly, ponies spend considerably more time chewing per unit of food consumed. For instance, where a horse may make between 800 and 1,200 chewing movements per kilogram of concentrate, a pony may make anything between 5,000 and 8,000 movements in order to consume the same amount of concentrate. This may possibly reflect the pony's adaptation to survive on very poor quality fibrous foods.

While it is desirable that fibre particles are reduced to less than 2mm (⅛in) in length during chewing, inspection of dung has revealed fibrous material up to 4cm (1½in) in length. This indicates that mouth processing is not completely effective.

Table 3.1 Chewing rates for consumption of chopped fibre by Thoroughbreds

	Length of fibre (cm)	Chews per kg dry matter	Consumption rate (grams/hour)
Long	33	3,351	1,364
Medium	11	4,200	849
Short	4	5,326	821

Table 3.2 Chewing rates for consumption of chopped fibre by Shetland Ponies

	Length of fibre (cm)	Chews per kg dry matter	Consumption rate (grams/hour)
Long	33	10,460	523
Medium	11	15,830	366
Short	4	12,500	417

THE STOMACH

The horse's stomach is small, comprising less than 10 per cent of his total gut volume. In order to reach it, food must pass down the oesophagus (the tube which links the mouth to the stomach). While the length of the oesophagus is of course proportional to the size of each individual horse, it can be very long, 1 to 1.5m (3 to 5ft) on average. It follows that if the oesophagus becomes blocked near to the entrance of the stomach, it can be extremely difficult to resolve the problem; beet pulp can be particularly problematic in this respect. The entrance to the stomach is controlled by a strong mus-cular valve known as the cardiac sphincter. This valve will allow matter to pass into, but not back out of, the stomach, and it can withstand considerable pressure to accomplish this. As a result, regurgitation of food or gas rarely occurs, and the horse is physically prevented from being able to belch or vomit. This can lead to serious colic should abnormal amounts of gas be produced, and in severe cases the stomach may rupture, a condition characterized by the horse taking up a dog-sitting pose and in which the gut contents are seen coming out of the nostrils.

The two most important things to bear in mind when considering the feeding of a horse are the small size of the horse's stomach and his continual feeding behaviour. While the stomach rarely completely empties, food material remains there for a short period of time; no more than three hours, on average. Food entering the stomach stimulates the emptying process, so when feeding stops the stomach stops emptying. A popular misconception is that if the horse drinks after feeding the stomach contents will be 'washed out', and it is the reason why many horse owners – mistakenly – do not allow their horses to drink after feeding. The truth is that ingested water follows the curvature of the stomach wall, passing into the beginning of the small intestine (the duodenum). Therefore very little water actually mixes with the stomach contents, making 'washing out' highly unlikely.

When food arrives in the stomach it stimulates the release of gastric juice. This occurs at a low level, but because it is occurring continually, the total daily production can be as high as 32 litres (7 gallons). The arrival of food in the stomach is also associated with an increase in acidity, although to a certain degree this is controlled by the flow of saliva produced during mouth processing. It follows that within the stomach there are marked variations in the degree of acidity:

- At the entrance the material is neutral.
- In the main part of the stomach it is slightly acidic.
- At the exit it is very acid.

Some fermentation occurs in the first and middle parts of the stomach, which leads to the production of lactic acid. The highly acid environment near the exit to the small intestine stimulates protein digestion,

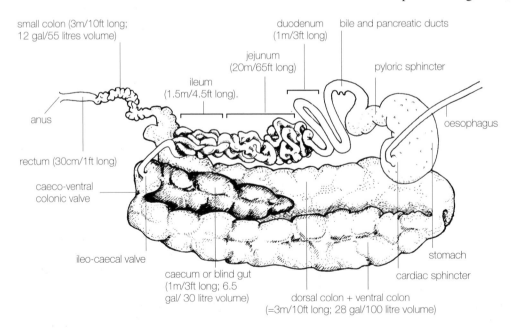

small colon (3m/10ft long; 12 gal/55 litres volume)

duodenum (1m/3ft long)

bile and pancreatic ducts

jejunum (20m/65ft long)

pyloric sphincter

ileum (1.5m/4.5ft long).

anus

oesophagus

rectum (30cm/1ft long)

caeco-ventral colonic valve

ileo-caecal valve

caecum or blind gut (1m/3ft long; 6.5 gal/ 30 litre volume)

dorsal colon + ventral colon (=3m/10ft long; 28 gal/100 litre volume)

stomach

cardiac sphincter

Fig 9 The horse's digestive system.

although this is limited by the stomach's small size and the limited time that the food is contained therein.

THE SMALL INTESTINE

The small intestine is composed of three parts: the **duodenum** which leads away from the stomach to the **jejunum** and then on to the **ileum**; it then joins with the hind gut which is the large intestine. Although the small intestine is on average around 20m (65ft) in length, food particles can still pass through quite rapidly; in just over an hour in fact. In this short period of time, non-fibrous material can be substantially digested.

The pancreas is a very important related gland which has two principal functions: one is the control of glucose metabolism, mediated via insulin; the other is the production of pancreatic juice which contributes to the breakdown (degradation) of food materials. Similar to gastric juice, pancreatic juice is continually produced at a low level. The presence of food within the stomach stimulates the production of large amounts which can total 20 litres (4.5 gal) over a 24-hour period. A release of bile from the liver and secretions from the pancreas are stimulated when material containing acid flows from the stomach into the duodenum. The release of these two agents rapidly neutralizes this acidity, which is important if the enzymes within the small intestine are to function properly.

The horse does not have a gall bladder and therefore bile cannot be stored; nevertheless it is continually produced. Bile has a high content of salts which results in the emulsification of any fat that is present in the small intestine. The enzyme lipase then sets to work, effectively hydrolysing this fat so that it may be absorbed and utilized. In spite of the relatively short time that food materials are exposed to enzymatic attack, most, if not all of the dietary fat is broken down and absorbed before it reaches the large intestine.

Horses seem to be very effective at digesting fat and it is now common practice to add vegetable oil to horse diets. There is evidence to indicate that this has a beneficial glucose-sparing effect in horses performing sustained aerobic work such as endurance horses, thereby delaying the onset of fatigue. However, if the fat supplied is not immediately used as an energy substrate, it will be stored as body fat.

In contrast to the limited breakdown of protein within the stomach, quite a lot is digested in the small intestine. Obviously this does not apply to the poorer quality proteins such as those present in lignified forage; most of those broken down in the small intestine will be quality feed protein. Starches are of great significance as they often represent the greater proportion of energy reserve in the horse's ration. Unfortunately though, starch is chemically complex and difficult to disarrange which can make it a problem to digest. Cooked starch is far more easily digested, hence the popularity of micronized and extruded products (*see* Chapter 9). Should a lot of starch escape degradation within the small intestine, it may then be rapidly fermented within the large intestine; such a situation results in excess lactic acid which may in turn lead to complications such as laminitis and colic. Since the starch content of grass is very low, horses are, not surprisingly, less well adapted to its digestion, so large meals that are rich in starch are not to be recommended.

THE LARGE INTESTINE

Inevitably some protein and starch will escape degradation in the stomach and small intestine, and so will arrive in the large intestine needing further processing. Added to this, micro-organisms, secretions into the gut and other substances such as cell debris acquired during the passage through the stomach and small intestine, will represent additions to the food that was originally ingested.

The component parts of the large intestine which are responsible for further processing are the caecum, and ventral and dorsal colons (which together comprise the large colon), the small colon, and the rectum. Together these components account for around 60 per cent of the total gut volume.

The Caecum

When food passes out of the small intestine it first reaches the caecum, a large, blind sac where food is fermented. In a mature 450kg (19cwt) horse, it is about 1m (3ft 3in) long, having a capacity of about 30 litres (6½gal); it accounts for around 15 per cent of the total gut volume. To enter the caecum, material must pass through the ileo-caecal valve, which is adjacent to the exit valve (known as the caeco-colonic valve), so material enters and leaves the caecum at nearly the same place. Once material leaves the caecum it passes into the ventral colon. The caecum and large colon contain the highest population of micro-organisms and in particular the cellulose-digesting bacteria. Although these organisms are present further along the tract, the primary sites for cellulose breakdown are the caecum and large colon.

The Large and Small Colon

The large colon is just over 3m (10ft) long and represents about 30 per cent of the total gut volume. The different parts of the large colon are separated by bends or flexures which reduce any backflow of material. Food residues move from one compartment to the next with very little mixing between compartments. Conversely, while material is contained within a compartment, considerable mixing occurs. Gas removal is facilitated by such active intestinal movement, and large volumes (up to 150 litres/33gal) may be absorbed; some may also be expelled via the anus. Parts of the dorsal colon can be as much as half a metre (20in) in diameter, before it reduces in size to join the small colon. The latter is about 3m (10ft) long and represents around 10 per cent of the total gut volume; it terminates in the rectum which is only 30cm (1ft) long and thus has limited storage capacity.

Onward passage of food to the rectum is increasingly resisted as material passes through the large and small colons, such that large food particles are held back. The purpose of this resistance is to ensure that the micro-organisms have had sufficient time to ferment the plant celluloses and hemicelluloses, the major food materials remaining after predigestion in the stomach and small intestine. While the bends and flexures of the colon certainly benefit the horse in terms of digestive efficiency, they can have horrendous consequences when things go wrong, such as in the event of impactions.

MICRO-ORGANISMS

In Chapter 1 we saw how the horse evolved to form a mutually beneficial relationship with micro-organisms (known as symbiotic microflora) which are capable of breaking down and fermenting plant cell-wall material. Now we will discuss how these micro-organisms contribute to the horse's well-being, and in addition how the quantity and nature of the food materials given to him affect the micro-organisms themselves.

The effectiveness of the fermentation system depends upon a *continuous* supply of raw material of the *same* type. Different microbes need different raw materials on which to flourish and grow. Thus, if the nature of the raw material supplied changes, say, from oats to hay, then this will favour the growth of hay-preferring organisms and see a decline in oat-favouring ones. Therefore when a horse's diet alters it can take some time before optimum numbers and hence optimum fermentation is achieved. It follows that the horse's diet should remain constant so that the popula-

tion of the appropriate micro-organisms will remain high and fermentation will be at its most efficient. This will in turn benefit the horse because it will produce a regular supply of the end-products of fermentation which are utilized by the horse.

The horse benefits in three ways from the presence of micro-organisms within his gut:

1. He can digest material such as cellulose which would otherwise be unavailable.
2. Micro-organisms synthesize essential amino acids and are themselves degraded to form a protein source.
3. Micro-organisms produce water soluble vitamins (B group) and vitamin K (fat soluble).

In order to ferment the substrate, these micro-organisms secrete enzymes; however, there are much larger organisms known as protozoa which can engulf food particles in order to digest them. It is not completely understood how effective the horse's large intestine is at absorbing nutrients and digesting microbial protein, and it is thought likely that many nutrients are simply lost in the faeces. The quality of food protein offered to a horse is therefore an important consideration, particularly for those animals which are still growing.

Where horses are fed to an unnatural pattern, such as those fed three times a day rather than *ad libitum*, there will be a fluctuation in the microbial population of the large intestine (remember, the effectiveness of fermentation relies on a continual supply of food). This fluctuation will reflect a change in the availability of nutrients, and associated with

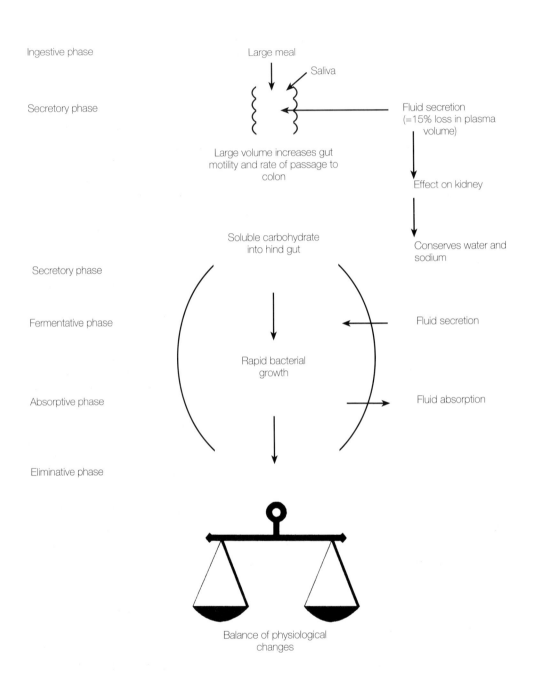

Ingestive phase

Large meal

Saliva

Secretory phase

Fluid secretion
(=15% loss in plasma
volume)

Large volume increases gut
motility and rate of passage to
colon

Effect on kidney

Soluble carbohydrate
into hind gut

Conserves water and
sodium

Secretory phase

Fermentative phase

Fluid secretion

Rapid bacterial
growth

Absorptive phase

Fluid absorption

Eliminative phase

Balance of physiological
changes

Fig 10 Factors affecting the balance of digestion. The delicate balance of physiological changes are upset by: overfeeding; sudden dietary change; chronic disease (parasitism); altered feeding intervals; salt and water deprivation.

this can be changes in the acidity of the gut contents. Thus, frequency of feeding can have a considerable effect on both hind gut function and the occurrence of digestive disorders. The overall digestibility of the feed may be little altered, although the well-being of the animal can be seriously jeopardized!

In summary, changes in the ratio of, say, hay and cereal can have both a qualitative effect on the species of microbe present in the large intestine, and a quantitive effect on the overall number of organisms present. Obviously the horse's digestive system takes time to adapt itself to what is being consumed, which is why any dietary changes must be made gradually over a long period of time. This is also why a hay-fed horse that is suddenly given grain may develop colic, laminitis or both. Similarly, the provision of a considerable amount of forage to a concentrate-adapted horse can lead to impactions in the hind gut. Thus as well as making changes gradually, it is clear why horses should have continuous access to foodstuffs of the same type, so that microbes in the large intestine are always exposed to the same environment.

The optimum goal of feeding a horse is that each mouthful of food should contain the same foodstuffs and thus nutrients, thereby promoting a constant microbial population. A grazing horse in the 'wild' would experience little qualitative difference between mouthfuls ingested throughout each day. Already some owners are providing 'complete' diets to their horses and seeing the benefits, and this does seem to be the logical way forward.

Products of Microbial Degradation

While we have discussed how microorganisms contribute to the horse's well-being, we have not yet seen what products are produced by microbial degradation of fibrous foods or how these products are used. In the large intestine, the volatile fatty acids (VFAs) – known as acetic, proprionic and butyric acids – are produced, the proportions of which depend upon the raw materials which are fermented. These VFAs are carried in the bloodstream to the liver where they are used as energy sources by the horse. However, more efficient energy usage is achieved if the horse can degrade carbohydrate in the small intestine and absorb sugars directly as energy substrates, rather than wastefully fermenting them to VFAs. Feeding large quantities of starch to a horse fed at set times can result in an incomplete breakdown within the small intestine, with a resultant 'spill-over' into the large intestine. This poses a possible danger of conditions such as laminitis, because starch can be fermented very rapidly by microorganisms in the large intestine and this may lead to catastrophic changes in the acid/base balance of the gut contents.

DURATION OF DIGESTION

It takes on average about seventy-two hours for all waste materials of a meal to be discharged, with food spending up to seventy hours of this time in the large intestine alone. The precise rate of passage will depend upon the nature of the diet; pelleted diets travel quicker than unprocessed feeds, for example. As a result, particles from a concentrate meal will begin appearing in the faeces earlier than those from a roughage meal. While the total time crossing the gut may be similar, 50 per cent of a concentrate diet may pass through in thirty hours, while the same proportion of a roughage diet may take forty-five hours.

Summary Points

- The horse is solely dependent on his teeth to process fibrous food materials finely.
- Considering the relatively short time that food materials are exposed to enzymatic attack, most, if not all the dietary starch (non-fibrous carbohydrate) is still broken down and absorbed before it reaches the large intestine.
- The horse possesses a symbiotic microflora which enables him to digest fibrous plant material which he cannot otherwise degrade.
- Horses digest young plant material far more effectively than mature herbage, whether this be fresh or conserved.
- Micro-organisms within the horse's large intestine contribute significantly to meeting his need for nutrients.
- Inappropriate feeding management can severely impair the horse's ability to extract nutrients from foodstuffs.
- Horses are less well adapted to the digestion of starch, so large 'starch-rich' meals are not to be recommended.
- The horse's health can be compromised by microbial malfunction.
- The micro-organisms in the horse's large intestine are adversely affected by sudden changes in diet.
- The risk of metabolic disease in the horse can be minimized by the provision of a uniform diet fed *ad libitum* since this will encourage a constant population of micro-organisms within the large intestine.

4

NUTRIENTS &

THEIR ABSORPTION

In earlier chapters we have seen how the horse is able to digest food by a combination of:

1. A simple system of breaking down non-fibrous food materials that relies on enzymes produced by the horse.
2. A complex fermentation system where fibrous food breakdown relies on the activity of micro-organisms.

Whether the horse relies on his own secretions, or on the activity of micro-organisms to aid digestion, depends wholly on the type of diet fed to him. Basically the horse's diet is governed by the purpose for which he is kept. For instance, a racehorse fed little fibrous food will depend largely on his own digestive secretions, whereas the non-working, field-kept horse will be heavily dependent on micro-organisms present in his large intestine.

Having established the two ways in which food can be digested, we now need to have a greater understanding of where

in the gut this food is absorbed and how it is utilized.

SITES OF ABSORPTION

Nutrients are not absorbed throughout the length of the gut; most are taken up between the stomach and the small colon (*see* Table 4.10). In the small intestine, glucose and other simple sugars are absorbed, as are the breakdown products of food protein: amino acids and peptides, for example. Fatty acids and glycerol are also absorbed in this area, as well as fat- and water-soluble vitamins. It is interesting to note that most of the calcium consumed is absorbed at this site, but only small amounts of phosphorus, and so these two important minerals do not compete for absorption sites.

Products that are not absorbed in the small intestine pass on to the large intestine where they may be absorbed, or

Table 4.1 Proportion of nutrients digested and absorbed in different parts of the horse's gut

Nutrients	Small intestine (%)	Caecum and colon (%)
Protein	60 – 70	40 – 30
Soluble carbohydrate	65 – 75	35 – 25
Fibre	15 – 25	85 – 75
Calcium	95 – 99	5 – 1
Magnesium	90 – 95	10 – 5
Phosphorus	20 – 50	80 – 50

NB: Small intestine is probable 1° site for fat and vitamin absorption.

more likely broken down further, especially nitrogenous compounds and carbohydrates. Other products absorbed in the large intestine include the electrolytes:

- Phosphorus: 75 per cent entering the large intestine is absorbed.
- Sodium and chloride: nearly 100 per cent is absorbed.
- Potassium: 75 per cent is absorbed.

However, the absorption of these electrolytes is associated with a large flux of water. Electrolytes are discussed in more detail in Chapter 12. The absorption of water from the large intestine is crucially important for the proper functioning of the horse and his gut. The water content of the small intestinal contents is about 90 per cent, and the faecal water content varies between 60 and 75 per cent in normal horses. However, the type of diet fed can affect these values: for instance: a horse fed a high oat, low roughage diet will produce drier faeces than one fed solely on a high roughage diet. The picture is further complicated when we consider the different types of roughage available. Thus a horse fed alfalfa will produce drier faeces than one fed on timothy hay, and sometimes quite copious amounts of faecal water are expelled in addition to the normal faecal material.

The volatile fatty acids resulting from fermentation in the caecum and large colon are absorbed where they are produced.

ENERGY

Energy is available to the horse in several different forms. In the diet, it may be supplied as fat, carbohydrate or protein. It is also available from bodily reserves of glycogen stored in the muscles and liver, or from fat distributed throughout the horse's body.

Traditionally, carbohydrates have always been considered the main source of food energy, although it is now clearly recognized that fat can be a significant source of calories. Relying on protein as a source of energy is both senseless and uneconomic since it is usually expensive, and the nitrogenous by-products of digestion are an embarrassment to the horse and his owner! Furthermore, the excretion of excess nitrogen can affect water balance and involve the wasteful expenditure of food energy. Since liver and muscle glycogen reserves are usually only required during periods of high energy demand, and bodily fat reserves are only mobilized if the horse reaches a state of being underfed, it is clear that carbohydrates provide the necessary day-to-day energy supply for most horses.

Types of Carbohydrate

Simple carbohydrates are broken down to glucose which is absorbed from the small intestine. Complex carbohydrates, as found in fibrous plant material, are fermented in the large intestine by micro-organisms, producing VFAs. These diffuse across the wall of the large intestine into the bloodstream for carriage to the liver. The horse can therefore have two quite separate energy supplies and the balance of the two will reflect the nature of the diet. For instance:

1. The horse in very hard work receiving 30 per cent roughage and 70 per cent concentrate will depend largely on digestion in the small intestine, with glucose the most available energy source.
2. The horse being maintained on hay will receive little glucose since grass is usually very mature when cut, so most of his energy needs will be met by VFAs produced in the large intestine. In this case the horse is almost wholly dependent on vigorous, healthy gut flora to maintain an energy balance.

Grass-fed, as opposed to hay-fed horses, will have both glucose and VFAs as energy sources since young growing grass can contain quite high levels of soluble carbohydrate. ('Modern' grasses such as hybrid Italian rye grasses can contain well in excess of 20 per cent soluble carbohydrate.) Such high levels have been incriminated as the cause of laminitis in horses turned out to grass in the spring.

Digestible Energy

While all foods contain energy, its availability to the horse depends upon the nature of the food containing it. For example, oats may contain the same energy (gross energy) as timothy hay, but the oats' energy is more available or digestible, and therefore in energy terms they are a more valuable feed source. The digestibility of the organic matter of the food material governs how much of it may be assimilated, and the fibre content which dictates how easily this is achieved, if at all. (*See* Table 4.2.) Consequently, high fibre foodstuffs – straw, for example – are poorly digested, so a lot of the food energy is unavailable to the horse and simply passes out in the faeces; in the case of straw, more than 50 per cent of the food energy will be present in the faeces. However, faecal energy losses can represent anything from 60 per cent down to as little as 20 per cent of the food value.

If we subtract the figure for the faecal energy loss from the food's original energy value, its digestible energy can be calculated easily. This value is extremely important and is used as the basis for all horse and pony diet formulation. The digestible energy of a food can be categorized into low, medium and high energy, and it is clear that if a horse is fed poorly digestible feed he will need to eat far more in order to maintain his condition than if he were fed highly digestible food in the first place. Obviously, when energy demands are high it is therefore impractical to use foods of low digestible energy content.

Glucose and other Simple Sugars

Glucose is probably the best source of energy for the horse's tissues, and the level of blood glucose is well controlled. The level that is maintained depends on the type of horse: ponies have a lower normal value than horses; Thoroughbreds have the highest level of all.

Absorbed glucose is carried away when the portal venous system drains the small intestine. Following a meal, therefore, the horse's blood glucose will rise steadily. It will peak at around four to six hours after a feed, only returning to normal resting values after a further period; perhaps up to two hours in ponies, although more rapidly in Thoroughbreds (*see* Fig 12).

The horse's tissues need glucose for muscle contraction; when this happens some of the absorbed glucose will be used up. However, unless activity is great, an excess will become apparent in the blood. To combat this the horse secretes insulin, which works to regulate the blood glucose, returning it to normal 'resting' levels (*see* Fig 13). The time taken to return to the resting value is commonly referred to as the 'tolerance time' and there is an important difference between horses in their ability to tolerate a glucose load, or starchy feed. Hot-blooded horses have a higher tolerance than their cold-blooded companions;

Table 4.2 Effect of fibre content on the amount of food digested by herbivores

Feed	Fibre content (g/kg dry matter)	% Feed digested	
		Horse	Cow
Maize	24	89	90
Oats	120	69	70
Pasture grass	180	64	81
Hay (early cut)	220	58	67
Hay (late cut)	300	52	59
Wheat straw	410	21	42

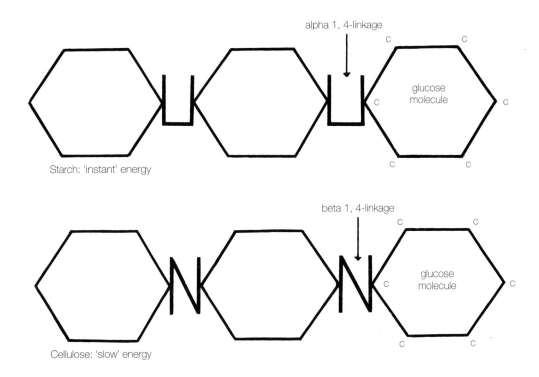

alpha 1, 4-linkage

glucose molecule

Starch: 'instant' energy

beta 1, 4-linkage

glucose molecule

Cellulose: 'slow' energy

Fig 11 Glucose molecules. Each molecule is made up of six carbon atoms (c). The way in which the molecules are linked determines whether the glucose makes starch (cereal sugars) or cellulose (plant sugars).

ponies demonstrate a lower production of insulin in response to feeding, which in practice makes them insulin insensitive. In other words ponies are less sensitive to insulin (*see* Fig 14), and their insulin activity seems to be less, although of course they will adapt to diet. It is suggested that this insulin insensitivity represents an adaptation to poor diets, so ponies can better withstand starvation than Thoroughbreds. This characteristic probably stems from a time when ponies had to exist in harsh conditions, where due to their dependence on a high fibre diet, glucose availability was low. This may mean that native ponies which still live in their natural environment are potentially hypoglycaemic (have low blood sugar).

In response to the presence of insulin, blood glucose is converted to fat reserves, or to muscle or liver glycogen. These glycogen reserves are necessary for the athletic horse as they allow him to sustain prolonged exercise and so compete successfully. Such reserves are not necessary for the native pony or cold-blooded horse, which may be another reason why such horses and ponies are insulin insensitive. In their case, excess energy will merely be stored as fat. As regards racehorses, due to their high grain diets, glucose represents a large proportion of the available energy; this can be seen as peaks and troughs in blood-glucose levels, reflecting the frequency of feeding. In contrast, horses fed roughage alone will have a more constant level of blood glucose.

As well as the quantity of insulin secreted and the horse's sensitivity to it, the rate of feed consumption also has an effect. As hard feeds are consumed more rapidly than roughage, grain-fed horses at peak blood-glucose level are more energetic (the infamous heating effect of con-centrates?). In order to try to reduce the discrepancy between peaks and troughs in blood-glucose values, the horse needs to be fed smaller meals on a more regular basis; so the old rule of feeding little and often is still as important as it has ever been.

While insulin seeks to regulate blood-glucose levels, there are other hormones which enable the use of glucose by the body. Vigorous work can create huge demands for energy – up to forty times that needed for resting activity for example – so when blood glucose can no longer meet this need, hormones are released which are a catalyst to the breakdown of glycogen to glucose, thereby supplementing blood supplies. Working a horse results in higher levels of muscle glycogen and circulating levels of

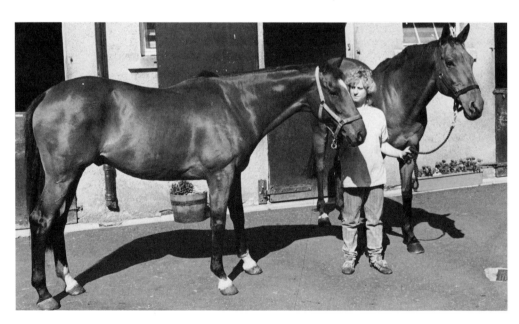

It is suggested that because of their sensitivity to insulin, Thoroughbreds are less able to withstand food reprivation than are ponies.

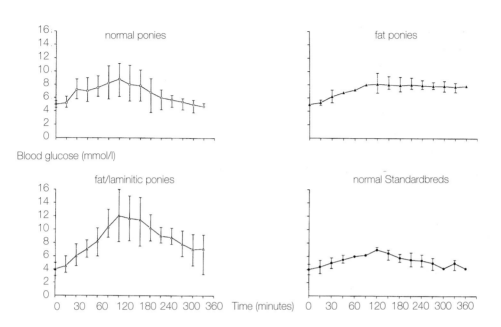

Fig 12 Mean (+/- sd) blood glucose values after oral glucose loading
(1g per kg bodyweight) in 12 ponies and Standardbreds.

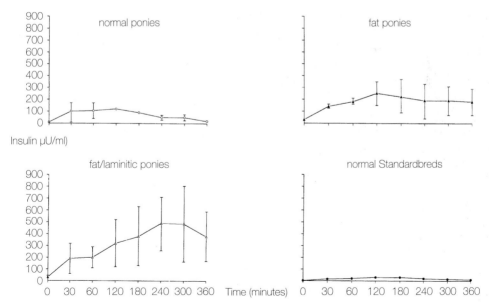

Fig 13 Mean (+/- sd) plasma insulin levels in 12 ponies and Standardbreds
after glucose loading (1g per kg bodyweight).

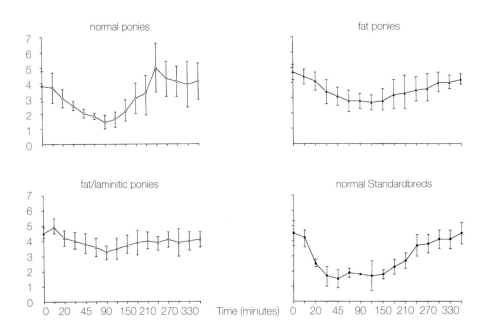

Fig 14 Mean (+/- sd) blood glucose values after intravenous insulin administration (0.4 iu per kg bodyweight) in 12 ponies and Standardbreds.

blood glucose. Exhaustion occurs when blood glucose falls below normal, and low glucose values are generally associated with exercise intolerance. Time of feeding is important in relation to work performance. If peak insulin production coincides with the time at which the horse is worked hardest, glucose levels will be adversely affected, as will the tolerance to work.

Volatile Fatty Acids (VFAs)

Acetic, proprionic and butyric acids are the most important VFAs which result from fermentation within the large intestine as they are the primary energy sources of the roughage-fed horse. Like glucose, VFAs can be used directly as energy sources. Pro-

prionic acid can be converted to liver glycogen and both acetate and butyrate contribute to the formation of body fat, so the roughage-fed horse does not lose out against his grain-fed counterpart, providing he is worked appropriately. Since the brain depends on blood glucose, it is essential that a suitable level is maintained. To do this, the horse existing on a high roughage diet needs to be able to produce glucose from a non-carbohydrate source, since dietary glucose supplies, or glucose precursors such as starch, will only be present in minimal quantities. Roughage-fed horses may therefore become adapted to producing glucose from either VFAs, fats or proteins. This can be advantageous, especially to horses undertaking endurance work,

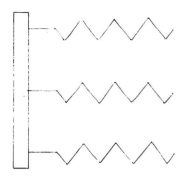

Fig 15 Structure of triglyceride fats (containing two and a half times the energy value of carbohydrate).

because the horse which can adapt to mobilizing fat thereby delays the onset of fatigue. Where a horse is conditioned to relying on VFAs, he will be more able to withstand periods of food scarcity since he can more readily mobilize his reserves. While starchy feeds may provide more 'instant' energy, fibrous feeds provide more 'slow-release' energy. Thus VFAs represent a more long-term energy supply which persists, as opposed to glucose energy which provides a short, powerful burst.

It should now be understood that the horse can use a range of substrates to provide the energy necessary for survival, and additionally for performance work. It is well known that the trained horse can improve his biochemical efficiency and can shift from one metabolic pathway to another in order to conserve glycogen reserves and to maintain blood glucose. Continuing muscle metabolism studies may tell us how we can keep our horses

running at full speed for longer periods of time by manipulating the combination of energy substrates that we feed. However, it may be a considerable time before someone finds out what gives some horses the 'will to win', while others are content to stop at the first hurdle!

PROTEINS

Proteins are complex organic compounds that are found in all living tissue. They are essential to life. Many different proteins occur naturally and they each consist of a long chain of amino acids, each link being represented by a single amino acid. (*See* Fig 16.) It is the sequence in which these links are formed together that endows the protein in question with its particular properties. One of the most recent and dramatic biochemical developments has been the ability to determine the amino acid sequences in genes which has enabled a better understanding of the inheritance of certain disease conditions such as cystic fibrosis.

Amino Acids

There are considered to be twenty-five amino acids of importance, of which ten cannot be made within the horse's body. A dietary supply is therefore necessary, and so these amino acids are described as 'essential' amino acids.

The demand for amino acids is regulated by physiological needs, so for example a young horse that is producing new tissues, or a mare feeding a foal, will have a higher demand than a mature horse that is merely

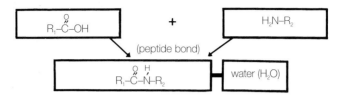

Fig 16 *Carboxyl group of one amino acid (R₁) joining like group of another amino acid (R₂), to form a peptide bond – the beginning of protein synthesis.*

replacing tissue. With regard to amino acids, plant protein is an important component of the diet, because plants (and some micro-organisms) can synthesize all the amino acids required by the horse. While micro-organisms are present in great numbers in the large intestine it is doubtful that much of this protein/amino acid supply is available to the horse as there is no system for digesting microbial protein in the large intestine. Therefore, as far as we are aware, the horse depends upon the protein he consumes for his supply of amino acids.

The picture is further complicated by manufacturers offering protein percentage levels on feed bags. This information can be very misleading since it does not indicate how much protein is truly digestible. For instance, shoe leather is high in protein, but it is indigestible! The quality of food protein is important for all horses and is crucial to growing foals, so you really do need to understand how much protein is *available* to your horse through his feed. For example, an old grass hay may be only 45 per cent digestible, whereas a 16.5 per cent protein dried grass may be 82 per cent digestible. It is, after all, only the digested protein which releases amino acids to the horse.

Apart from the problem of digestibility, there is also the quality of the protein itself to be considered (the relative quantities/balance of amino acids present). While the horse needs to be supplied with enough digestible protein, it also needs to be of the appropriate quality. Young growing foals and pregnant and lactating mares represent those horses with the highest requirements. Generally, animal proteins contain a better balance than vegetable proteins and of the latter, soya protein is the best.

Since the horse cannot store amino acids in the same way that he can store energy, and because amino acids are required in certain proportions to form specific proteins, any excesses of individual amino acids will be wasted. Amino acids may be wasted if:
1. They are present in the wrong proportions.
2. They are in excess to requirements.
3. Energy is in short supply.
It is inadvisable that amino acids act as energy sources. While they can be linked together with little expenditure of energy, their breakdown releases ammonia in the liver, which is potentially toxic. Although the ammonia is rendered harmless by conversion to urea, this process uses up energy

and thus heat is produced. Clearly this is undesirable in horses that are working hard, so for performance horses the ration should be finely tuned by ensuring that:

1. Digestible protein is supplied;
2. The protein contains the right balance of amino acids;
3. The correct amount of digestible protein is supplied.

In most feeds for horses, the amino acid most likely to be deficient is lysine, and dietary deficiency can impair the performance of horses with high protein requirements. While poorer quality proteins (available through the average hay- and oats-based diet) may be adequate for mature horses kept solely at maintenance, growing animals will require higher quality protein sources such as fishmeal or soya for optimum growth.

While it is scientifically accepted that providing dietary protein in excess to need is wasteful, common opinion also has it that excess protein predisposes horses to laminitis. However, there is *no* evidence to support this view, which has its origins in the idea that horses develop laminitis when fed lush grass, high in protein, in the early spring. In reality, it is more likely that the high levels of soluble carbohydrate present in young grass are fermented rapidly, causing an explosive increase in lactic acid, which begins the pathological process that results in laminitis.

Summary Points

- Absorbed glucose is either used directly; is stored in a readily available form (glycogen); or is stored as body fat.
- An understanding of how the horse uses the end products of digestion should lead to improved precision in feeding.
- Overfeeding protein, whilst unlikely to cause serious problems, is both biochemically inefficient and uneconomic.
- Because hay protein is usually of poor quality, hay-fed horses could benefit from the inclusion of some good quality supplementary protein.
- The horse can use a range of substrates to provide the energy necessary for survival and for performance work.
- The protein value of a diet to the horse depends on the quantity of protein it contains and its quality.
- Diets that contain poor quality protein must be fed in greater quantities than those containing better quality protein.
- Care must be taken when purchasing feedstuffs to ensure that the food has not been adversely affected by heating or other processing techniques.
- In view of the fact that lysine is likely to be deficient in common horse feeds (cereals and hay), attempts should be made to balance the amino acid supply to optimize liver function in athletic horses. (For example: alfalfa can be substituted for the concentrate to reduce the dependence on starch-rich foods where appropriate in regard to workload.)
- In contrast to what many people think, excessive protein consumption by horses does not lead to laminitis.

5
Minerals

When we talk about feeding a balanced diet we know that it should be one that provides all the nutrients a horse requires for good health and vitality. So far we have seen the importance of the necessary nutrients such as carbohydrate, protein and fat, but in order to ensure an appropriate diet for the horse we must take care that he also receives adequate vitamins and minerals. These are important for many bodily functions, ranging from proper hoof growth to ensuring normal hydration. It is thought that probably as many as forty or so minerals are involved in tissue function, although the quantities required of some of them are so minute that it is highly unlikely that a deficiency will ever occur.

The aim of the horse with regard to vitamins and minerals is that he is always in a neutral state: neither deficient nor over-supplied. For example sodium, potassium and chlorine are primarily concerned with the maintenance of acid/base balance. If the acidity or alkalinity of the horse's body changes far from neutral then the biochemical processes essential to life will malfunction. Similarly, minerals such as calcium and phosphorus have a well known structural role, so an abnormal level of them will lead to skeletal problems.

Some minerals fulfil a number of different roles, while others have unique functions. Minerals can also interact and while in some cases this may be beneficial, it can also cause problems. The total quantity of each mineral present in a feed can meet or exceed the horse's need, but excesses of one or more minerals can interfere with the way in which the horse metabolizes others. When formulating a ration it is therefore extremely important to be aware that mineral *imbalances* are just as crucial as simple deficiencies. Such imbalances can be created by an overuse of trace element supplements when the exact mineral composition of the basic diet is not known. The consequences of such imbalances are most serious in growing horses, when bone malformation can occur. Moreover, quite apart from excessive mineral addition causing imbalance, some minerals are themselves toxic, such that an oversupply can have dire consequences. Some essential elements, such as copper, are cumulative poisons and oversupply can lead to a gradual build-up in certain organs, notably the liver and kidneys. Fortunately the horse seems fairly resistant to copper poisoning, being able to withstand levels that can cause death in other species. Other elements such as selenium, fluorine and iodine, can be highly toxic. Thus mineral supplements must be designed with great care, firstly to rectify any deficiencies and secondly to adjust the overall mineral balance of the ration. The major failing of standard commercial supplements is that they cannot possibly balance all of the variable diets fed to horses.

MAJOR MINERALS

Calcium (Ca)

This mineral has the distinction of being the most abundant in the horse's body, with about 99 per cent being found in the skeleton and teeth. The remaining 1 per cent is crucially important, being involved in enzymatic activity, the conduction of nerve impulses, the coagulation of blood and muscle contraction.

Adult horses at maintenance require less calcium than growing foals or hard-working horses. The assumption for horses in work appears to be that calcium requirements increase in proportion to energy requirements. Working horse diets based on traditional feeding practices are grossly deficient in calcium and therefore unbalanced.

Green leafy crops, especially legumes, are good sources of calcium; cereals and cereal by-products are very poor sources. The conventional mineral supplement used for a calcium deficiency is limestone, but where phosphorus is also deficient, dicalcium phosphate and limestone may be added to rectify any deficiency. In young, growing foals calcium deficiency will be manifested by rickets, whereas in mature animals the bones will decalcify and spontaneous fractures may occur. During training, considerable bone remodelling occurs, but the impact of this on calcium requirements has not yet been established.

Phosphorus (P)

Some 80 per cent of the total body phosphorus is located in the skeleton and teeth of the horse, in close association with calcium. Phosphorus has many functions in the horse's body, with a vital role to play in energy metabolism. A mare's milk, too, is rich in both calcium and phosphorus, therefore a lactating mare will require substantially more calcium and phosphorus to sustain the minerals lost through feeding a foal. The phosphorus requirements of working horses are considered to be related to energy needs, thus a horse in hard work requires considerably more than one at maintenance.

Green leafy materials are poor sources of phosphorus and this is also the case with conserved roughages. Cereals contain a lot of phosphorus, so it is unlikely that a horse fed a lot of concentrates will ever be deficient; indeed the most likely problem in this case will be an excess. This leads to the absorption of calcium being reduced, thus causing a deficiency. Where bran is fed in combination with cereals the problem will be further compounded, because 1kg (2.3lb) of bran contains merely 1g (0.03oz) of calcium, but 12g (0.4oz) of phosphorus; thus substantial amounts of limestone would be needed to correct this imbalance. Far better not to feed bran, and so not have an excess of phosphorus in the first place! Too much phosphorus leads to chronic calcium deficiency and a condition known as nutritional secondary hyperparathyroidism, or Miller's disease, bran disease, or 'big head' as it is more commonly known.

Magnesium (Mg)

Magnesium is closely associated with both calcium and phosphorus and thus, not surprisingly, about 70 per cent of body magnesium is found in the skeleton. The remainder is in the soft tissues and body fluids where it functions as an activator of enzymes and is therefore involved in many essential processes. Naturally good sources of magnesium are vegetable protein concentrates (soya for example), dried yeast, bran, and legumes such as alfalfa. The mineral supplement most frequently added to the horse's diet is magnesium oxide, sold commercially as calcined magnesite. This material is not very palatable and it is advisable to conceal its presence in sweet, highly palatable materials such as molassed sugar beet pulp.

It is inadvisable to feed excess magnesium to horses because it has a laxative effect. Most horses' daily need for magnesium would easily be provided by hay, although foals may need supplementation. Recently there has been some interest in the role magnesium plays in diets for working horses, and it has been suggested that the incorporation of fat into the diet increases the need for magnesium. Requirements for horses in training are related to energy needs, with a horse in full work requiring about 15g (0.5oz) of magnesium daily. A ration of 4kg (8.8lb) hay, ½kg (1.1lb) of bran and 8kg (17.6lb) of oats would supply about 18g (0.6oz) daily, so on such a diet no supplementation would be necessary.

Potassium (K)

Potassium has a major influence over body fluid regulation and in the maintenance of the horse's acid/base balance. It is also concerned with carbohydrate metabolism and the function of nerves and muscles. It is unlikely that a grass-kept horse would ever be deficient because plant materials contain very high levels of potassium. Cereal grains contain much lower levels, however, and the potassium intake of stabled horses will be much lower than those kept at grass. Horses are in fact naturally adapted to consuming vast amounts of potassium and these are excreted via the kidneys very rapidly, providing there is an adequate water intake. The highest requirement for potassium would come from a horse in hard work, but since 4kg (8.8lb) of hay alone would meet the need of such a horse, a potassium deficiency is extremely rare.

Sodium (Na)

Sodium is the most important electrolyte involved in the maintenance of acid/base balance, and in the regulation of body fluids. It is found in body fluids such as blood plasma, and is responsible for the salty taste of blood. Sodium is involved with the transmission of nerve impulses and the absorption of sugars and amino acids from the gut. Most of the sodium consumed by horses is in the form of sodium chloride (common salt) and when it is lost from the body it is mostly in this form. Foods of vegetable origin have a relatively low sodium content while those of animal origin contain much more. Thus, horses at grass will ingest low levels of salt and this is perfectly acceptable because losses from the body will also be low. It is only when horses are exercised hard that they sweat and lose sodium. Such horses will require supplementary sodium which can be supplied as a free-access rock salt/salt lick, salt in the diet or as a component of a compound feed. During intense work the degree of sweat loss is affected by fitness, the nature of the activity, adaptation and environment. Thus it is impossible to be dogmatic in terms of specifying the working horse's need for sodium, and provided copious amounts of water are available, it is unlikely that the horse will ever consume too much salt.

Horses in hard work fed the traditional diet of hay and oats will be deficient in sodium by at least 20g (0.7oz) and thereby require a minimum supplement of 50g (1.8oz) of salt daily. It is foolish to allow a sodium deficiency to occur since it can markedly affect the horse's performance. Dehydration can occur quite quickly, even if sweating may seem less profuse and less obvious, such as at low humidity and with a stiff breeze blowing. A 'pinch test' can be used to detect decreased skin elasticity which is indicative of dehydration, although by such time the horse is quite badly affected – so prevention is certainly better than cure. Obviously it is a sensible precaution always to have free-choice salt available and to incorporate it into the diet of hard worked horses.

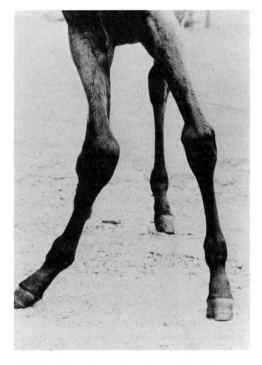

Epiphysitis and angular limb deformities in a Thoroughbred foal.

Chlorine (Cl)

This element is associated with sodium and potassium in acid/base control and body fluid regulation, and is frequently overlooked. Apart from these important functions it is also a component of the bile salts and is necessary for the formation of hydrochloric acid, a gastric secretion necessary for digestion. It may be lost from the body in urine and also in combination with sodium and potassium in the sweat. It is generally accepted that providing the sodium requirements of the horse are met, then so will those for chlorine.

Sulphur (S)

In spite of the important role of sulphur, the sulphur requirements of horses have not been established since it is assumed that its intake would be in the form of protein, and it is expected that the horse will never be protein deficient. However, horses in hard work, which are being fed just oats and 'hard' racehorse seed hay, may be marginal for protein. Those horses with the highest requirements will be lactating mares and young, rapidly growing foals.

TRACE MINERALS

We have now seen how calcium, phosphorus and magnesium fulfil important structural roles, and how sodium, potassium and chlorine are needed for acid/base balance and fluid regulation. However, the horse still requires other essential elements in order to control his metabolic processes: these are known as trace elements because their concentration in the horse's body is far less than that of the major minerals.

Iron (Fe)

Iron is widely distributed in foods (including plants) and so it is highly unlikely that a horse would ever be deficient. Good sources are green leafy materials, legumes, cereal offals, straw and many animal-based feeds such as fishmeal. The most important iron containing protein is *haemoglobin* which contains about 60 per cent of the total body iron, followed by the muscle protein, *myoglobin* at 20 per cent. Some iron is stored in the spleen, liver, kidneys and bone marrow as 'ferritin'. A further storage form is haemosiderin, The storage and transport forms of iron make up 20 per cent of the total iron content of the horse.

The horse has a low requirement for dietary iron because iron produced from the destruction of haemoglobin is recycled and made available for the synthesis of 'new' haemoglobin; it is estimated that only 10 per cent of it escapes this recycling. Forages and cereal by-products provide more than the horse will need, thus the horse will consume excess iron. It is noteworthy that iron concentration can be depressed by oversupplying copper, manganese and zinc, so over-enthusiastic mineral supplement users should take note! *Iron supplements are unnecessary.*

Unfortunately many horse owners, and racehorse trainers especially, will not believe this, insisting that low haemoglobin values reflect a shortage of iron. It has been demonstrated experimentally that various iron supplements under normal feeding regimes were *ineffective* in improving both haemoglobin levels and the oxygen-carrying capacity of red blood cells. However, horses still get iron preparations injected and included in their feed. What *is* of concern is that excess supplementation with iron has been shown to depress both serum and liver zinc, and we do not know what subclinical effects there may be as a result. While chronic iron toxicity can result in reduced growth and impaired trace element metabolism, acute toxicity can occur through over-enthusiastic oral dosing. Young foals are particularly susceptible and deaths have been recorded in foals given oral iron preparations. Finally, if you must use an iron supplement, check that it is ferrous rather than ferric iron; the latter is largely unavailable.

Manganese (Mn)

There is very little manganese within the horse's body, and this small amount is found in the bones and the organs such as the liver and kidneys. Of particular importance for horses is the role of manganese in activating the enzymes necessary for cartilage formation. Requirements for horses have not yet been established, although it is considered to be unlikely that they would ever be deficient because the element is widely distributed in foodstuffs and roughages. However, although a dietary deficiency is unlikely, it is important to be aware of the possible interactions. Thus excess liming of pasture or feeding of calcium can depress manganese availability, and in view of its role in activating the enzymes necessary for cartilage formation, it *may* be involved with the limb abnormalities and contracted tendon problems of neonate foals.

Zinc (Zn)

This is present in every tissue of the horse's body and is concentrated in the bones rather than the liver. It is found in reasonably high concentrations in the skin and hair coat. Zinc has a very important biochemical role in the horse: it activates enzymes and is a component of many others, and thus is involved with their diverse functions throughout the body. It is widely available in feeds, and animal by-products and yeasts are very good sources. Recent studies suggest that higher levels than originally thought are necessary to minimize the incidence of metabolic bone disease in young, fast-growing Thoroughbred foals. Horses appear to be tolerant to quite high levels of zinc; however, excess zinc supplementation in young stock has been shown to cause bone abnormalities due to induced copper deficiency. This emphasizes that while high zinc intakes *per se* may not be toxic, they may induce a secondary deficiency.

Another factor to be aware of is that high dietary levels of calcium can induce a zinc deficiency if zinc intakes are marginal. Unsupplemented diets for performance horses can be marginal for zinc, whereas both manganese and iron are frequently present in excess; thus there is a need for supplementing zinc to balance these excesses. Zinc deficiency is often characterized by abnormal skin conditions and it is thought to have an important role in hoof horn formation.

Copper (Cu)

Copper is present in all body cells, and accumulates in the liver if an excess is fed. Although not a constituent of haemoglobin, it is essential for its formation: if copper is in short supply, the horse's ability to absorb, metabolize and use iron in haemoglobin synthesis will be impaired. There are several copper-dependent enzymes which are concerned with vital processes, such as oxygen metabolism. It is also necessary for normal pigmentation of hair. There is good evidence to show that in copper deficiency, bone disorders occur, and that horses are very tolerant to high dietary levels of copper. Thus it would appear that supplementary copper may be provided without risking toxicity. However, it must be remembered that excess copper will interfere with both zinc and iron metabolism, so it is crucially important to ensure the correct balance is maintained.

Cobalt (Co)

This element is required in minute amounts and is an integral part of vitamin B_{12} (see Chapter 6). There is no record of cobalt deficiency in the horse, and the horse has the amazing capacity to remain in good health on cobalt-deficient pastures where cows and sheep would lose condition and eventually die if cobalt were not supplemented! Apart from its role in B_{12}

synthesis, cobalt also activates certain enzymes. There is no evidence to indicate that supplementing cobalt is of any benefit to the horse.

Iodine (I)

The only known role of iodine in the horse is in the synthesis of the two thyroid gland hormones which regulate basal metabolism. Since so little iodine is required, the use of iodized salt ensures no deficiency occurs; normal horse diets contain sufficient iodine. Problems may be seen in the foals of deficient mares: while the mare may display no clinical signs, her foal may show classical signs of goitre (swelling in the neck due to enlargement of the thyroid gland), as well as other clinical signs of iodine deficiency. However, goitre can also arise through over-supplementation, so care must be taken to differentiate the cause of the goitre in case supplements are mistakenly given to horses suffering from toxic goitre.

Selenium (Se)

This is a very necessary, yet very toxic element. Its significance was first realized some forty years ago, when its involvement with muscle function and vitamin E was recognized. It is a component of an enzyme which detoxifies peroxides that attack cell membranes. Deficiency is unlikely and there are few recorded cases amongst horses in the UK. Interest currently centres on the role of both selenium and vitamin E in the high performance horse where it is felt that supplementation with selenium may be beneficial. It has been suggested that the element has a preventative role to play in 'tying-up syndrome', although this has not yet been substantiated. Supplementary forms of selenium such as sodium selenate contain high levels of available selenium, but due to its toxic nature care must be taken not to oversupply the element.

Summary Points

- While deficiencies of magnesium, potassium, chlorine and sulphur are unlikely, sodium deficiency is very common. It is also highly preventable!
- Although the horse can apparently tolerate excessive intakes of most trace elements (except selenium and iodine) it is inadvisable to over-supplement individual elements because of the well established interactions that take place between them.
- There could be subclinical effects which need only reduce performance by 0.001 per cent for a horse to lose a race.
- In addition to over-supply of individual elements, it is important to remember that the overall balance of minerals should be maintained. In a practical feeding situation, first check the adequacy of the supply and then balance the ration.

6

VITAMINS

Vitamins are active substances, essential for life as they ensure the correct operation of a horse's physiological functions. They are organic compounds required in very small amounts in the diet. While the horse can synthesize some vitamins, either by microbial activity in the caecum or by normal function of an organ (renal production of vitamin D, for example), it would be unwise to assume the horse to be vitamin self-sufficient since we know little about his ability to produce them.

Vitamins are put into two groups: fat-soluble and water-soluble. As their name implies, fat-soluble vitamins are soluble in oils and fats, and are insoluble in water; they can be stored in fatty tissues and organs like the liver and kidney. Water-soluble vitamins are removed by the kidneys from the circulating blood, such that quantities which are in excess to immediate requirements are excreted in the urine. Thus there is very little storage of water-soluble vitamins, but in contrast, large quantities of fat-soluble vitamins can be stored. It is this fact which makes it imperative not to over-supplement with these vitamins.

FAT-SOLUBLE VITAMINS

The fat-soluble vitamins are A, D_2, D_3, E and K, and although the discovery of vitamins dates from the beginning of the twentieth century, the role of cod-liver oil in the prevention of rickets has been known for a longer time.

Vitamin A

At the turn of the century, a yellow pigment called carotene was found to be present in many fats, oils, vegetables and fruit, and it was shown to be essential for life. Fish-liver oils were shown to produce the same beneficial dietary effects as carotene, and the active ingredient was found to be a carotene-related alcohol named 'vitamin A'. Thus you can supply a horse with either carotene or preformed vitamin A to the same effect. Substances such as carotene are described as provitamins or vitamin precursors (that which a vitamin is converted from). Carotene contained in plant material is absorbed from the horse's small intestine and partially converted into vitamin A in the cells of the wall of the small intestine; the rest is converted in the liver.

The most active form of carotene is generally considered to be ß-carotene, although other forms do exist. The efficiency of ß-carotene conversion to vitamin A varies according to the vitamin A status of the horse. If there are excessive stores of vitamin A in the liver (through extended exposure to high, fresh grass diets) or high circulating levels of A (due to over-supplementation) then the efficiency of conversion will be less. It has been suggested that a horse can 'switch off' ß-carotene absorption from the gut when excess is supplied and when the horse is replete with vitamin A.

Excess vitamin A causes toxicosis (known as hypervitaminosis) which leads to weight loss, bone decalcification, haemorrhage, poor coat/skin condition and increased heart rate; death may result from acute toxicosis. Chronic hypervitaminosis A interferes with the function of other fat-soluble vitamins, notably vitamin D. Thus particular care will be needed in the formulation of diets for growing horses where the correct balance of nutrients is essential for bone formation.

Vitamin A is involved in several essential body functions. These are:
- Visual processes. The horse's eye is a different shape from ours, and he has to move his head to focus (*see* Fig 17). Furthermore, the positioning of the eyes enables limited binocular vision but extensive monocular vision (*see* Fig 18), which means that the horse can keep most of his environment under scrutiny.
- The function and maintenance of the epithelial tissues and mucous membranes; these surface tissues harden and degenerate if a deficiency occurs.
- Metabolic processes within cells and

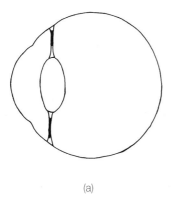 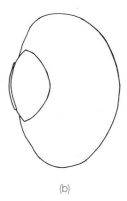

(a)   (b)

Fig 17 Comparison between the eyes of the horse and the human: (a) human; (b) horse.

thus deficiencies will interfere with cell replication and obviously growth.

- The reproductive processes and mare fertility.
- The production of antibodies and thus disease resistance.

Carotene and vitamin A are particularly susceptible to destruction through oxidation, which is accelerated by sunlight, moisture and heat. Small quantities of trace minerals such as copper (*see* Chapter 5), contribute to biodeterioration. Losses may therefore occur during processing to form cubes and the like.

Vitamin D

The use of cod-liver oil as an effective treatment for rickets has already been mentioned, but it was not until the early 1900s that the particular agents involved were separated and identified. Two compounds are recognized as having curative effects on rickets: vitamin D_2 (ergocalciferol), derived from vegetable material and vitamin D_3 (cholecalciferol), of animal origin. The formation of vitamin D requires ultra-violet irradiation which contributes to the destruction of vitamin A and carotene. No feed ingredients that are *commonly* used in the manufacture of horse compound feeds contain any vitamin D, although precursors may be present. Small amounts may be present in sun-cured roughages and fish offals. Thus stabled horses excluded from sunlight require supplementation.

Vitamin D plays a crucial role in the metabolism of calcium. The absorption of calcium from the small intestine is promoted by vitamin D, and therefore in its absence little is taken up. Deposition and mobilization of bone calcium is controlled by vitamin D, so that blood calcium levels are maintained. Vitamin D is intimately involved with calcium and phosphorus metabolism, and there exist interrelationships with sodium, potassium and magnesium.

Any deficiency will have far-reaching effects on bone metabolism. Demineralization of bone will occur, leading to rickets in foals and osteoporosis in adult horses. Insufficient dietary supplies of

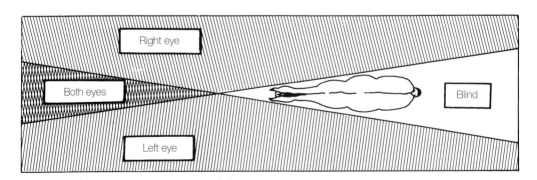

Fig 18 Visual field of the horse.

calcium and phosphorus can have similar effects (*see* Chapter 5). Excessive supplies of vitamin D lead to excessive uptake of calcium and consequently very high blood calcium levels. The excess may be deposited in blood vessels, the heart, bone joints, wall of the intestine and so on, which necessarily reduces the elasticity of the horse's tissues. In severe cases, heart failure may result and at the very least, the horse's ability to exercise will be severely jeopardized.

Vitamin E

The most active form of vitamin E is alpha-tocopheral acetate. This is the name that is frequently printed on supplement tubs or on labels attached to bags of horse compound feed that contain *added* vitamin E. Fresh green roughages are good sources of vitamin E. Grass loses vitamin E during the normal hay-making process, although little is lost through ensiling or in the making of bagged grass or big-bale silage.

The major function and best recognized property of vitamin E is the prevention of oxidation of material within and between the cells of the body (antioxidant activity). Unsaturated fats within the cells of the horse's body are particularly susceptible to oxidation, and if this occurs, tissue damage may result. The more active the cell, as in the muscles of an exercising horse, the greater the inflow of fat to meet energy demands and thus the greater risk of tissue damage if vitamin E is in short supply. Antioxidant activity is also important for the stability of red cells and the integrity of the small blood vessels. Vitamin E is present in all tissues and organs of the horse; it is essential for the maintenance of the endocrine (hormonal) system, and it promotes the production of hormones that stimulate output from the thyroid and the adrenals; it has no specific role in the reproduction of the horse.

A dietary deficiency may lead to muscle lesions (myopathy), and if heart muscle is affected, then heart failure may occur. The involvement with musculature is crucial to the exercising horse, and it has been suggested that vitamin E deficiency may be involved with tying-up syndrome.

Selenium is closely associated with the functions of vitamin E (*see* Chapter 5, final section), and to some extent they are interchangeable. Since the effects of vitamin E are largely 'invisible', the consequences of supplementation are difficult to evaluate, although we are aware of some factors that increase the need for vitamin E. Currently it is common practice to supplement horse diets with fat, and in particular those diets destined for the endurance horse.

Horses fed roughages grown in selenium-deficient areas will have higher vitamin E needs. Stress imposed by overcrowding, poor ventilation, transport and disease is also alleged to increase the horse's need. In this context it is of interest that vitamin E has been linked with disease resistance in the horse. It has been suggested that where disease resistance may be crucial, the addition of a minimum of 150mg vitamin E per kilogram of feed will minimize the effects of disease challenges to the horse.

Vitamin K

Vitamin K can be produced by single-cell organisms in the large intestine of the horse, but it is unresolved whether or not this material is available to him; therefore he may, or may not be independent of a dietary source. Fresh leafy roughages are a very good source of vitamin K, whereas dried and processed products of vegetable origin possess very little vitamin K activity. The only function that has been described for vitamin K is that relating to the blood-clotting mechanism: where there is a deficiency, blood will not coagulate properly, which means that minor injuries can bleed indefinitely leading to death, and spontaneous haemorrhage can also occur. In contrast to other fat-soluble vitamins there is little body storage, and so daily supplies of vitamin K are necessary.

WATER-SOLUBLE VITAMINS

As their name implies, these vitamins are soluble in water, and are therefore only stored to a limited extent in the body. Quantities in excess to immediate requirements are rapidly removed via the kidneys. The best known water-soluble vitamins are those of the B-group (or B-complex) and vitamin C. There are also a number of organic compounds which have vitamin-like activity, although their need has not been totally established and there is debate as to whether or not they are true vitamins. Their metabolic roles are still being investigated.

Vitamin C

Also known as ascorbic acid, this vitamin has an important role first recognized hundreds of years ago by sailors. They discovered that the onset of scurvy could be prevented by consuming fresh fruit, and in particular citrus fruits such as limes and lemons. Horses, unlike humans, can produce their own vitamin C from glucose in the kidneys. Vitamin C is important for cellular function, body defence mechanisms and iron metabolism. If horses can produce their own vitamin C then why should they require supplements? Under certain conditions it is possible that the horse is unable to produce enough of the vitamin to meet his own needs. For example, very young foals take some days before their synthetic system is fully operational. In older animals it has been suggested that their synthetic ability can be compromised for a variety of different reasons, including stress factors such as heat, cold, parasites, noise, infection, overcrowding, inadequate ventilation and transport.

Horses fed conserved roughages and concentrates will receive no dietary vitamin C and will be totally dependent on production within their bodies. Vitamin C is extremely expensive and very unstable in the presence of alkalis, metals such as copper, also heat and moisture, and is therefore better supplied in a supplement rather than in a compound feed.

B-Group Vitamins

These are active co-enzymes and their presence is required for the formation of enzymes; in their absence, biochemical reactions are blocked. These co-enzymes are involved in many activities and reactions, but their full role has yet to be evaluated. For example, pantothenic acid is part of co-enzyme A, and in this form is involved in excess of one hundred reactions in the horse's body. The B-group vitamins are categorized as follows:

Thiamine (vitamin B₁) The vitamin is produced by single-cell organisms in the caecum of the horse and it appears that sufficient is absorbed from food sources to meet the needs of horses existing in fairly 'natural' conditions. However, there is good evidence to suggest that stabled, high performance horses require supplementation. Most vegetable products contain some thiamine.

Thiamine is crucially important to the performance horse because it is involved with enzyme systems that release energy from absorbed or stored carbohydrate and fats. It is also involved in neural activity, and deficiency can result in quite dramatic clinical effects. A variety of substances possess anti-thiamine activity thus destroying any thiamine present. Such substances will induce a deficiency in the face of apparent dietary adequacy, so beware. Due to its neural involvement, thiamine is alleged to have a 'calming' effect on excitable horses, but there is no scientific proof of this.

Riboflavin (vitamin B₂) This vitamin is also synthesized in the caecum and large intestine, although we do not know how much, if any, is absorbed. Grass-fed horses will certainly be well supplied since grass contains a plentiful supply. Cereals and their by-products contain little, while some animal products are good sources (dried milk for example), and dried yeast is an excellent source.

Riboflavin, is involved as a co-enzyme in a number of important biochemical pathways. It permits enzyme systems associated with carbohydrate, amino acid and fat metabolism to function, and so it is intimately involved with energy release. It is also essential to normal growth and health; as a result, deficiency symptoms tend to be non-specific. In foals we might expect nerve degeneration, dermatitis and possibly some light sensitivity, or conjunctivitis. Newborn foals will be particularly dependent on dietary supplies until the microflora in the large intestine become well established. High energy diets, such as those fed to performance horses, will directly affect riboflavin requirements because the raw materials used are very low in the vitamin. Furthermore, a low fibre diet will mean that the microflora in the hind gut will not be very active and thus they will produce small quantities of riboflavin.

Mouldy feed contains mycotoxins which inhibit the transportation of riboflavin from the site of absorption in the gut wall to the liver and other organs. Thus poor quality feed will increase the need for this vitamin.

Pyridoxine (vitamin B₆) This vitamin is essential for both the horse and the microorganisms contained within his gut. It is incorporated into enzyme systems involved in a large number of metabolic processes, and it is estimated that over fifty different enzymes depend directly on it. It is closely involved with amino acid metabolism, energy production, activity of the central nervous system, fat metabolism, haemoglobin production and the synthesis of globulins (proteins which carry antibodies for disease resistance). A deficiency produces non-specific symptoms; however, skin and blood changes are likely, poor growth is to be expected, and there may be nervous symptoms ranging from irritability to convulsions. Foals and youngstock generally have a high requirement, and in the adult horse it is unlikely that caecal synthesis in the hind gut will be of benefit.

Some medicinal products antagonize pyridoxine activity: for example, sulphonamides have been shown to interfere, and a substance called hydracyanine acid – found in linseed and possessing antibiotic properties – is opposed to pyridoxine.

Cobalamin (vitamin B₁₂) Cobalamin is unique in that it is the only vitamin to contain a mineral element, cobalt. Another important feature is that it is of animal origin, a fact recognized when it was originally named, 'animal protein factor'. It assists in the metabolism of fat, carbohydrate and protein, the latter activity being the most important. It is involved in several enzyme systems which mostly deal with single-carbon units; these are the basis for protein formation. It is also closely associated with folic acid, and with the production of the amino acid methionine. This sulphur-containing amino acid is of course very important for foal growth and the production of the hard protein keratin that is found in the hoof horn.

Cobalamin is absent from vegetable-based diets, and deficiency may be recognized in horses by neural and blood changes as well as depressed growth. 'Megadosing' with cobalamin is practised by some horse owners; no toxicity or side effects have been reported at high dose levels so far. It is not excreted rapidly and many of the horse' organs are capable of storing it, with 30–60 per cent of reserves being held in the liver. It is excreted via the kidneys and in the bile. Its activity is opposed by high levels of niacin or by oxidizing agents, but its uptake from the gut is improved by calcium, copper and iron. Cobalamin itself improves the uptake and utilization of carotene from the intestine and the functioning of vitamin A.

Cobalamin is an expensive nutrient only to be found in animal products and supplements; it is rapidly destroyed by UV light.

Niacin (vitamin B₃) Niacin is widely involved in metabolism and particularly in energy-release processes. It can be produced by the microflora in the hind gut, although little will be absorbed, and also from the amino acid tryptophan. This latter process is suppressed by fat and thus will be limited in endurance horses receiving a lot of dietary fat. It is thought that plant sources of niacin are poorly available to the horse and that it is rapidly lost from the body, with a third of the intake excreted within twenty-four hours. A common deficiency symptom is dermatitis.

Pantothenic acid This vitamin is involved with the metabolism of fatty acids, the formation of antibodies, neural function and energy metabolism. Horses do not benefit from bacterial synthesis in the intestine so are totally dependent on dietary supplies. Little is stored, and excess supplies are rapidly excreted. It is normally provided in supplements as calcium pantothenate, and it appears that vitamin C can partly compensate for a deficiency.

Biotin This vitamin is well known for its role in hoof horn formation. Its full biochemical role is not yet fully understood, but it has involvement with the metabolism of carbohydrate, fat and protein. It affects protein synthesis, and controls the rate of production and deposition of the scleroproteins (hard proteins such as keratin).

Biotin is involved with the maintenance of epidermal tissues, so the first visible sign of a deficiency is usually dermatitis. A chronic deficiency is considered to be associated with poorly formed hoof horn; an acute deficiency would interfere with energy metabolism, leading quickly to death.

Horses depend on dietary supplies of biotin since microbial synthesis is unlikely to provide for the horse's need. Very little is known about the true requirements for biotin, particularly in relation to horn growth. It seems that there is not a simple relationship between the two and that other nutrients are also required, in particular protein, calcium and sulphur. Good horn development is therefore dependent on an adequate supply of nutrients rather than on biotin alone.

Folacin This name is used to refer to a group of compounds, the best known being folic acid which was first extracted from spinach.

These substances are important in nitrogen metabolism. Micro-organisms can produce folacin, although there are doubts over the effectiveness of caecal synthesis in the horse. Sulphonamides interfere with the metabolism of folacin which is closely linked to vitamin B_{12}. Shortages of B_{12} lead to a secondary loss of folacin which can be alleviated by the amino acid methionine; a deficiency of iron aggravates the situation. Folacin levels are very low in cereals, so supplementary folacin may be beneficial to horses in hard work.

VITAMIN-LIKE SUBSTANCES

Choline This substance is essential for fat metabolism and is involved in the transmission of nerve impulses. It is found throughout the cells of the body, and is manufactured by the gut microflora. It is widely available in horse feeds. It is difficult to imagine that a deficiency could occur.

Carnitine This compound fulfils an important function in muscle, and research at the Animal Heath Trust in the UK has shown that it is beneficial to the exercising horse. It depends on the presence of other water-soluble vitamins, and assists in fat and carbohydrate metabolism.

Pangamic Acid (vitamin B₁₅) It has been claimed that this contributes to horse performance and that endurance is increased. It is involved with fat metabolism and prevents the excessive accumulation of fat in organs and blood vessels.

Bioflavanoids These were originally extracted from paprika and are claimed to have an antihaemorrhagic effect; they may therefore be of possible benefit to horses prone to bleeding. Many racehorses are known to suffer from this problem.

Summary Points

- Fat- and water-soluble vitamins are very important to the horse's well-being.
- Vitamins A and D are frequently overfed in practice, and vitamin E is underfed, both because of its cost and possibly because its importance to the horse is not fully realized.
- While a deficiency of vitamin E may occur, it is very unlikely that deficiencies of A, D and K will be seen in horses.
- The activities of the most important water-soluble vitamins are intimately related.
- Unlike fat-soluble vitamins, water-soluble vitamins can be overdosed without the risk of toxicity.
- Any deficiency can be readily made up by dietary supplementation, although this may prove expensive.

7

GRASSLAND

In their natural state horses spend around sixteen hours a day grazing, and as we saw in Chapter 3, they are very selective grazers. Rather than simply grazing a patch until all available food is consumed, they will roam vast distances in search of what they deem most suitable. Thus during the daylight hours they are continuously ingesting small amounts of herbage and are therefore correctly termed 'trickle' feeders.

The extensive grasslands grazed by the horse's predecessors were generally of low quality, containing a vast range of different grass species and herbs. This active grazing behaviour and the poor quality herbage prevented the horse from becoming obese, and in winter he would probably have been in moderate to poor condition depending on the prevailing weather conditions. The diversity of the vegetation over a range of different soil types would have ensured these horses consumed the range of nutrients necessary to support their different physiological states of pregnancy, growth, lactation and so on.

CONSEQUENCES OF DOMESTICATION

In all cases domestication has led to a restriction in the horse's environment, by placing him either in a restricted area such as a paddock, or a stable. As a result he is now dependent on us to provide a suitable supply of herbage. In addition, due to the imposed restriction on his roaming instinct, we must also ensure adequate exercise. Associated with this restriction of movement is the fact that droppings become concentrated over a small area, and therefore the burden of parasites is much increased. Moreover horses defecate in limited areas of the pasture, such that these become latrines. This concentration of natural fertilizer leads to vigorous plant growth, but as horses will not graze near their own droppings this plant material remains unharvested, becoming long and fibrous. Such areas are known as 'roughs', and the grazed areas are referred to as 'lawns' because they are so closely grazed.

In the absence of grazing management, these roughs will increase in size from

Some Poisonous Plants and Shrubs

Yew	White bryony
Hellebore	Hemp
Columbine	Rhododendron
Monkshood	Horsetail
Larkspur	Bracken
Poppy	Sowbread
Greater celandine	Pimpernel
St John's wort	Thornapple
Corncockle	Henbane
Soapwort	Deadly nightshade
Sandwort	Foxglove
Chickweed	Ragwort
Lupin	Lily of the valley
Laburnum	Fritillary
Cowbane	Black bryony
Hemlock	Darnel
Water dropwort	

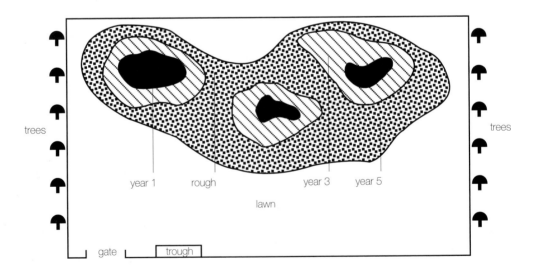

Fig 19 *The appearance and development of roughs in pastures grazed by horses.*

year to year, reducing the size of the lawns. (*See* Fig 19.) As a consequence the lawns will become overgrazed, so although the paddock might seem quite large in terms of hectarage, the productive grassland may be only very small; it has been demonstrated that as little as 10 per cent of a long-established pasture may be grazed. Thus casual inspection of a field may show plenty of grass, but a closer inspection will probably reveal that it is only present in the undesirable roughs. Overgrazing of lawns will lead to the disappearance of useful plant species and an invasion of weeds and grasses of low productivity. Furthermore, it is likely that the intake of worm eggs and larvae will increase, and that greater soil ingestion will occur – up to 1 or 2kg (2 to 4lb) of soil a day may be eaten by a 500kg (10cwt) horse.

AGRICULTURAL DEVELOPMENT

The revolution in agriculture has seen a change in farming practices: first the enclosure of the land; and second, the need for an increase in productivity from the land to support more animals. As a result, the basic foodstuff which once contained a diverse plant population, has changed in nature, low quality grasses giving way to high quality ones which have high yields per hectare and are of high nutritional value. The mid-eighteenth century saw the introduction of timothy grass to the UK, and more recently we have witnessed the development of a whole range of hybrid grasses whose composition is dramatically different from that of the original grass species grown in the UK. Some of these 'modern' grasses contain only low levels of essential minerals, but high levels of soluble carbohydrate.

Another change of great significance to the feeding of horses has been the ploughing up of permanent pasture to grow cash crops. Nowadays pastures are ploughed up and reseeded on a regular basis, the new crops more commonly being called 'leys', and containing only a few grass species; even if your horse is grazing permanent pasture it is very likely that his winter supply of hay will have been made from a ley. Thus grass, the basic feed for all our horses, is now totally different from that which was fed centuries ago, and in most cases today contains only a few different species. Fig 21 shows the common grass species to be found in pastures or hay.

It is most important that you learn to recognize these grasses as there are large differences in their feed values, and this will affect their ability to meet your horse's requirements. Table 7.1 shows a comparison of their composition and feed value at the same stage of growth; from this it is apparent that timothy, cock's-foot and fescue are poorer quality grasses more similar in composition to the traditional grass species that were available to horses on extensive grazing years ago.

In plant materials energy may be present as starch, fibre or water-soluble carbohydrate, but in grasses it is only contained in fibre and water-soluble carbohydrate: there is no starch present. This is in direct contrast to cereals, where the bulk of the

White clover

Chicory

Comfrey

Garlic

Fig 20 Legumes and herbs commonly found in pasture or hay.

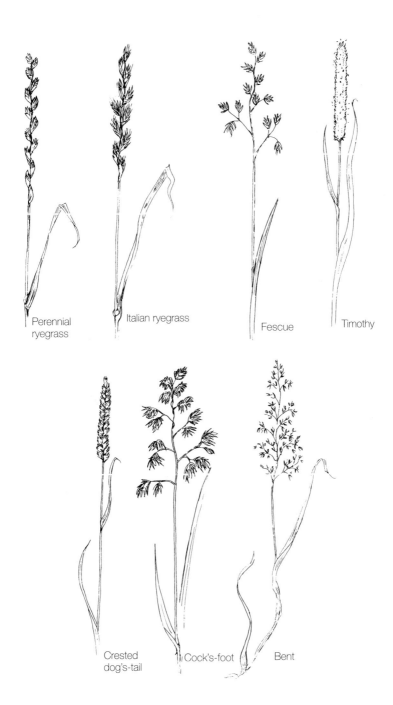

Fig 21 The grass species most commonly found in pasture or hay.

Table 7.1 Effect of type of grass on nutrient composition

Grass type	Protein	Fibre	Soluble carbohydrates
Timothy	16	35	6
Cock's-foot	14	41	9
Fescue	13	40	6
Perennial ryegrass	18	28	16
Italian ryegrass	19	26	24

energy is present as starch. Obviously in their natural environment horses did not eat starch-rich foods, so it is not surprising that so many digestive disturbances are encountered in horses fed large quantities of cereals.

'Modern' grass leys bring their own problems: while horses can readily digest the soluble carbohydrate found in grasses, within their natural environment their intake would have been low. In contrast, where horses are turned out onto lush pastures dominated by 'new' grasses such as Italian ryegrass which contain a high level of soluble carbohydrate, their intake can be high, in spite of the fact that they are trickle feeders. You will probably already be conscious of the dangers of this situation: excess soluble carbohydrate is quickly converted to lactic acid in the gut, and the increased acidity kills useful bacteria; this leads to the release of endotoxins from the bacteria which can cause severe circulatory disturbances. Provided the horse or pony survives the immediate cardiovascular stress then it is probable that laminitis will develop.

The problem for the horse of carbohydrate overloading at grass is exacerbated when fertilizers are used to encourage grass growth. Productive grasses respond by growing very quickly, so the horse may be presented with a large bulk of soluble-carbohydrate-rich herbage. This situation would never have been encountered in extensive grazing situations, and it is noteworthy that the native pony is particularly vulnerable to laminitis when grazed on improved grasslands. Prevention is always better than cure in regard to laminitis. This can be achieved by restricting access to improved grasslands and replacing it with poor quality fibrous feeds such as cereal straws.

GRASS GROWTH

Grass growth is regulated by climate. Low temperatures overwinter and drought in midsummer will inhibit its growth; at other times grass will flourish, providing it receives adequate sunlight and water. In the UK maximum growth typically occurs during May and early June (see Fig 22), followed by a midsummer slump, and then an increase during August and September; the excess in summer may be cut and conserved to provide food for the winter. In other countries the climate will also dictate corresponding patterns. Fig 22, gives an indication of seasonal grass production from well managed grasslands.

As a rough guide, one hectare (approximately 2.5 acres) will maintain four 500kg (10cwt) horses during peak growth, but during midsummer this will fall to two horses per hectare. Intensive grassland management incorporating the use of fertilizers and sprays can be very successful on large equine units where there is a high level of management. In these enterprises there are enough horses to graze the paddocks regularly and closely, so there is never an excess of lush growth which is

the thing to be avoided. This is the danger on a small unit where an over-enthusiastic application of fertilizer may result in excessive grass growth; horses which indulge themselves in this sort of pasture may then develop fermentative colic, laminitis or the like. The aim is therefore to strike a balance between the production and the utilization of grass so that the needs of the horses are met without prejudicing their health. In short, they are provided with just the right amount of grass for their needs – no more, and no less.

Unfortunately though, the seasonality of grass growth means that at some times of the year horses are short of grass, while

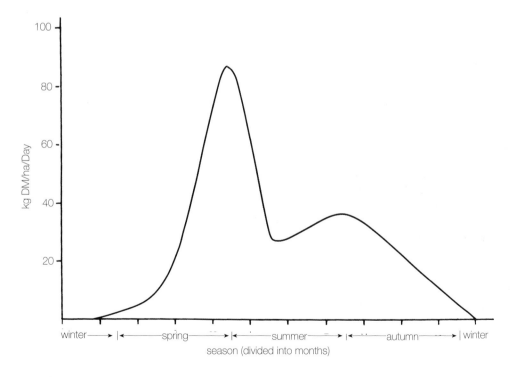

Fig 22 Seasonality of grass growth.

at others an excess is available. The horse has some inherent ability to control his intake so that it is relative to his need, but it is very imprecise. Consequently, nearly all horses and ponies at grass during the summer will over-eat simply because the grass is so available: being enclosed in a paddock they do not need to 'work' for their food by roaming to find it, all they need do is put their heads down!

While some of the consequences of over-eating can be quite dramatic, in any case it is undesirable for horses to put on excess weight as this will inhibit their 'work' performance. What we want our horses to do ranges from gentle hacking and Pony Club activities, to more rigorous sports such as eventing. But whatever our expectations, it should be obvious that excess weight is both a health risk and a handicap. So what should you do if you find yourself with too much grass? There are a number of ways to deal with this circumstance, although each has its problems as well as its benefits:

1. Mixed grazing of horses with sheep, cattle or goats.

There are three main problems with this solution:

a) The horses may chase the sheep, although they seem less likely to torment goats.

b) Post and rail fencing will not contain sheep.

c) Cattle rub against fences and destroy them.

However, there are also three main benefits:

a) The parasite load will be reduced.

b) The grass in the 'roughs' will be consumed (goats and cattle are best for

> **Grassland Management**
> The five main components:
> - Manuring
> - Mechanical treatment
>   Harrowing
>   Rolling
>   Topping
>   Reseeding
> - Conservation
>   Hay
>   Silage
>   Dried grass
> - Grazing
> - Drainage

this) and the overall productivity of the pasture will be improved.

c) A further income may be generated from rental grazing.

2. Increase the numbers of horses by taking in grass liveries.

The problems with this solution are:

a) Fighting between horses.

b) Uncontrolled bleeding due to such injuries.

c) Increased parasite load.

d) Increased areas of 'roughs'.

e) Responsibility for other people's horses.

f) Lack of uniformity in worming programmes.

g) Uncontrolled mating!

The benefit of an additional income seems unattractive in comparison to the problems.

3. Temporary/movable fencing.

The problems involved are:

a) The initial cost of the fencing.

b) Making it visible to horses.

However, the benefits are attractive:

a) You can adjust the grass supply to the needs of your horses and thus avoid over-eating.

b) Excess grass can be conserved.

c) You can graze the excess with other species, without mixing the two.

The last strategy is therefore probably the best solution because it has the benefits of the other options with none of the disadvantages. The capital cost of the fencing will soon be recouped, and the fencing will last for many years.

The picture below shows a paddock that has been well managed; it has been grazed alternately with cattle, a policy which has minimized the development of 'roughs' and, by adjusting the number of animals to the growth pattern of the grass, has prevented it from becoming too long and coarse. By comparison, the photograph overleaf illustrates the situation we so often see during the summer when horses are at grass: large areas of 'roughs', over-grazed 'lawns' and a large number of weeds with a predominance of buttercups. Note also the presence of ragwort.

GRASS QUALITY

Energy, protein and fibre are principally affected by the stage of growth of the

Well-managed horse grazing where the available grazing has been divided into paddocks.

Grazing pasture showing roughs and lawns.

grass. While the grass remains at the vegetative stage – that is, where no seed heads are visible and the grass is not readily identifiable – then it will have a high feed value. The production of seedheads enables easy identification; it also signifies a rapid fall in feed value. When young, most grasses have a high feed value because they are low in fibre and high in energy and protein. The poorer, less productive grasses lose feed value more quickly than modern grasses as they age. If the grass can be continuously harvested, either by grazing or cutting as it grows, then it will remain at a young stage of growth and be high quality. Where grasses are not adequately harvested in this way they will go to seed, which leads to an overall deterioration in the feed value of the pasture, which means in turn that it will support fewer horses. Horse pastures that are under-grazed will therefore deteriorate as the season progresses; it will be apparent from Fig 23 that as fibre levels increase (as the grasses age), the protein content falls. The most obvious deficiency

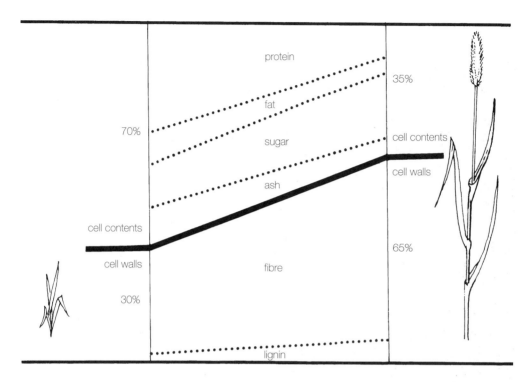

Fig 23 Effect of age on composition of grass plant cells.

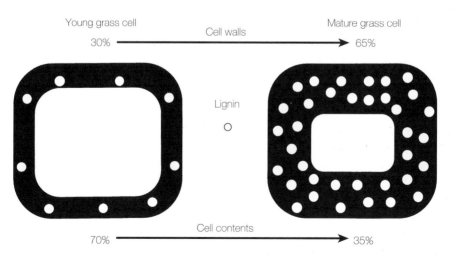

Fig 24 The effect of age on plant cells.

is of protein, although high fibre levels mean that less energy is available. Thus over a year, grazing horses may be confronted with the following extremes of herbage quality:

- Early season grass which is usually lush, low in fibre and rich in protein, and contains readily available energy sources (soluble carbohydrate).
- Mid- to late-season grass which is often fibrous, indigestible and low in protein and available energy.

These characteristics, coupled with the quantity of grass produced per hectare, will materially affect the number of horses that may be adequately kept on any one pasture.

How the pasture contributes to the horse's nutrient requirements for the remaining months may be assessed from Table 7.2. However, while the data contained in this table will give an overall view of what happens, in practice it should be treated with caution as there are so many variables which can affect individual pasture quality and productivity.

Nevertheless it becomes clear that in most cases, excess energy will be supplied throughout the grazing months, whereas protein will be supplied in great excess early in the season, and yet will be grossly deficient late in the season. However, this should not cause immediate concern, as the apparent protein deficiency will only be significant to growing and breeding horses. Mature horses doing little work will be able to tolerate a protein deficit for quite some time. At the other end of the scale, horses can tolerate very high levels of protein without apparent ill-effect. The excess energy available could, however, be more

Table 7.2 Contribution of grazing to horse requirements (value per hectare)

Month	No. of 500kg horses	% of energy requirement	% of protein requirement
April	1	180	320
May	4	180	286
June	3	160	220
July	$1\frac{1}{2}$	138	158
August	2	125	95
September	$1\frac{1}{2}$	110	63
October	1	100	60

(Figures based on a 500kg horse consuming 10kg dry matter per day, equivalent to 2% of liveweight.)
N.B. The seasonal conditions implied by the months noted are relevant to all climates similar to the UK's. Appropriate adjustments must be made for other climates.

of a problem as we know horses do not accurately regulate their intake according to their energy requirements. The only way to avoid unworked, mature horses or ponies over-consuming energy on good grass is by restricting their grazing time such that only about 1 per cent of liveweight is consumed at grass. Appetite must then be met by feeding low-energy dense feeds such as straw on a grass-free paddock.

Wintertime brings its own concerns. Although during the winter period horses appear to graze a pasture, their nutrient intake from it will be negligible. Furthermore, they will be actively damaging it by overgrazing; that is, eating the grass too short and making it susceptible to frost damage, and the resultant dying out of productive grasses will enable weeds and less productive grasses to invade the pasture. Inevitably there will also be damage to the grass by poaching during wet periods as the ground cover is reduced. Thus, horses and ponies should not be wintered on their summer grazing, but kept on free-draining, all-weather sacrifice areas, or wintered in providing they can be exercised sufficiently. Light winter grazing of horse paddocks with sheep will keep them tidy and fertilized and will give some control to the roughs.

Poaching in a gateway.

Micronutrients

In the 1950s some concern was expressed about the effect of the disappearance of herbs and weed species from pastures due to the use of sprays and the establishment of new leys. Scientists were unable to show any disadvantages in terms of the growth rates of cattle kept on modern 'improved' pastures as compared to the traditional permanent pastures, although they did not consider micronutrient status. However, some new horse farms in Kentucky are experiencing certain bone problems in

Table 7.3 Mean major mineral content (g per kg dry matter) of herbs, legumes and grasses
(Soil type, fertilizer application and stage of growth can affect these values.)

	Calcium	Phosphorus	Magnesium	Sodium
Herbs	19.7	8.1	12.5	2.0
(Chicory)	20.0	11.1	10.7	3.7
Legumes	23.7	8.4	11.4	1.0
(Alfalfa)	30.1	9.1	9.1	1.0
Grasses	5.4	5.6	4.0	1.7
(Timothy)	5.8	5.3	4.2	3.0

Table 7.4 Mean trace mineral content (mg per kg dry matter) of herbs, legumes and grasses
(Soil type, fertilizer application and stage of growth can affect these values.)

	Iron	Manganese	Copper	Cobalt
Herbs	358	42	10	0.19
(Chicory)	469	57	12	0.20
Legumes	306	45	9	0.17
(Alfalfa)	291	37	9	0.15
Grasses	264	29	8	0.15
(Timothy)	374	30	7	0.15

their young horses grazing recently established pastures. In the UK, there are figures available which compare the mineral contents of grasses, herbs and legumes; these are summarized in Tables 7.3 and 7.4, and perhaps go some way to explaining some of the problems encountered.

From the data supplied it is evident that both herbs and legumes are very good sources of calcium, and that furthermore, the ratio of calcium to phosphorus is between 2 and 3 to 1. Grasses, too, usually contain more calcium than phosphorus although the ratio is often much closer, perhaps 1.5 (or less) to 1. For good bone growth a calcium/phosphorus ratio of at least 2 to 1 is required. So better bone development will be expected in horses fed diets rich in herbs and legumes. Apart from the major minerals, both herbs and legumes are also very good sources of trace minerals; chicory, for instance, is an excellent source of iron.

When considering the horse's needs we should at all times remember that the horse is *not* nutritionally wise, so he will *not* select foods rich in nutrients that he lacks. However, it follows that horses grazing a pasture that contains a lot of legumes and/or herbs will be more likely to eat them as a matter of course, and thus benefit from their greater mineral content. There has been a recent trend to include herbs such as chicory, comfrey and garlic for example, in coarse mixes and other feeds; probably for their 'medicinal' properties, rather than their content of micronutrients. It is doubtful whether the quantities used would provide a meaningful supply of nutrients.

CONTRIBUTION OF GRASS TO HORSES' REQUIREMENTS

Well-managed, high quality grass will meet the micronutrient needs of horses at rest; pregnant and lactating mares; and horses that are still growing. This is hardly surprising, as originally horses in their natural

Table 7.5 Major mineral content (g per kg dry matter) of well-managed grass in comparison to animal requirements (g per kg dietary dry matter)

Nutrient	Content in grass	Maintenance	Pregnancy/ Lactation	Growth
Calcium	6.0	2.4	4.3	6.0
Phosphorus	3.5	1.7	3.4	3.5
Magnesium	1.7	0.9	1.1	0.8
Potassium	27.7	3.0	3.8	3.0
Sodium	1.9	1.0	1.0	1.0
Sulphur	2.0	1.5	1.5	1.5

environment were able to perform all of these functions on a forage-only diet. Tables 7.5, 7.6 and 7.7 relate the needs of these horses to the micronutrient content of grass.

Although vitamins D, B_1 and B_2 are absent from grass, this is of no consequence. Vitamin D will be synthesized in adequate amounts in the body of the

Table 7.6 Trace mineral content (mg per kg dry matter) of well-managed grass in comparison to animal requirements (mg per kg dietary dry matter)

Nutrient	Content in grass	Maintenance	Pregnancy/ Lactation	Growth
Iron	150.0	40.0	50.0	50.0
Manganese	102.0	40.0	40.0	40.0
Copper	8.0	10.0	10.0	10.0
Zinc	51.0	40.0	40.0	40.0
Selenium	0.05	0.1	0.1	0.1
Iodine	0.23	0.1	0.1	0.1
Cobalt	0.1	0.1	0.1	0.1

Table 7.7 Vitamin content of well-managed grass in comparison to animal requirements (per kg dietary dry matter)

Nutrient	Content in grass	Maintenance	Pregnancy/ Lactation	Growth
A (iu/kg DM)	30,000– 200,000	2,000	3,000	2,000
D (iu/kg DM)	–	300	600	800
E (iu/kg DM)	100–300	50	80	80
B_1 (mg/kg DM)	–	3	3	3
B_2 (mg/kg DM)	–	2	2	2

grazing horse provided there is adequate sunlight, and the B vitamins will be produced by the micro-organisms within the gut. However, nutrient deficiency can arise where the grass intake of the horse is limited. For example, in their natural environment mares will foal at the height of the grass-growing season when there is an abundance of grass. However, nowadays Thoroughbreds are encouraged to breed earlier in the year, when grass supplies are inadequate.

Work with a high energy requirement would have been alien to the horse in his natural environment: galloping would only have been necessary to avoid predators, and this would have entailed just a short burst of activity. Prolonged exercise whereby much of the sodium is lost would not have occurred, and thus grass sodium levels would have been adequate. We cannot expect horses performing hard work to thrive on a grass-only diet: apart from the fact that they would not be able to consume enough energy from grass, it would also be grossly deficient in sodium. Another possible consequence of the (stabled) horse performing hard work is the suggested need for additional B-complex vitamins. However, there is only limited evidence to indicate that the micro-organisms within the gut cannot produce enough under these management conditions.

Summary Points

- The horse in his natural habitat was a trickle-feeder, spending a long time each day selectively grazing herbage and travelling long distances.
- Few horses have the opportunity to graze land which supports a wide cross-section of plant species, including the wide range of herbs normally found in old pastures.
- Grazed herbage is the staple food for horses and ponies, but domestication of these horses and developments in agricultural technology have meant that the contribution of grass to the horse's diet has changed, and that now it can be both inadequate and dangerous.
- Where grazed herbage is the sole source of nutrients, it is important to appreciate that this supply will vary because there is a significant change throughout the grazing season both in terms of herbage yield and quality.
- Recognition of the above, and the adoption of a sensible grazing strategy, will ensure that your horse or pony receives sufficient nutrients.
- Well-managed grass can supply all the horse's need for trace minerals and vitamins, provided horses follow a natural breeding cycle and are not required to perform hard work.
- The result of good grassland management is that pasture production in future years will not be prejudiced.
- Once it is realized that modern grass leys do not necessarily contain the correct levels of all minerals to support rapid development or reproduction, appropriate supplementation may be implemented.

8

CONVENTIONAL FEEDS

ROUGHAGES

The terms roughage and forage are often used to mean one and the same thing, but this is incorrect. 'Forage' describes *all* food for horses, whereas 'roughage' specifically refers to the coarse, indigestible constituents of food which contain about 18 per cent or more fibre and thus provide bulk and satisfy appetite. Nowadays, several of the commercial products marketed as 'high fibre' feeds can hardly be described as fulfilling the role of roughage.

A rule of thumb has long been established that the horse needs to be supplied with a minimum of ½ to 1kg (1 to 2lb) per 100kg (220lb) of liveweight in order to keep his gastrointestinal tract fully operational – but is this truly the case? Horses and ponies are impressive in terms of the time and effort expended in chewing their food: horses may chew 4,000 times per kg of hay, and ponies may exceed this figure

by as much as three times. This results in most of the roughage being reduced to less than 4mm (³/₁₆in) lengths. Close examination of the faeces of hay-fed horses confirms that it is composed mostly of very small particles of matter, with but a few lengths of roughage 2 or 4cm (¾ to 1½in) long. From this it would appear that horses and ponies may be fed pre-ground roughages in pelleted form with no direct adverse effects to their 'physical' health: this means that the equivalent amount of hay can be safely fed in a nut form.

Pre-treatment of roughage in this way removes the horse's need to chew, which on average has been measured as one chew per second. Consequently the horse can ingest pelleted, ground fibrous foods very quickly; you will be aware of the difference in time it takes for a horse to eat 1kg (2lb) of nuts as opposed to an equivalent weight of hay! Such rapid consumption increases the risk of the horse choking, over-eating if large quantities are available, and – probably most important – developing stereotypic behaviour. This abnormal behaviour may manifest itself in a number of ways, but the most easily recognizable are weaving and crib-biting. This behaviour is considered to develop because the horse's drive to perform the normal eating pattern of prolonged bouts of chewing is frustrated. Thus, while roughage can be supplied in cube form without affecting physical health, it can be psychologically detrimental. Roughage provided in the traditional form as hay or the like is therefore preferable in order to reduce the risk of the horse developing abnormal behaviours.

Conserved Grass

The quality of conserved grass will primarily depend upon the state of the grass when it is cut, and secondly, on the treatment it receives after cutting. Prolonged drying of grass in the field may result in large losses of leaf and hence nutrients. This is best illustrated in Table 8.1, which compares methods of conserving grass with the resultant nutrient content. It is clear from the table that rapid conservation is beneficial in terms of safeguarding the nutrient content of the raw material. Grass hay alone is inadequate to support growth as it is deficient in calcium, phosphorus, copper and vitamin E. Moreover, prolonged storage results in the demise of vitamin A, so the dubious practice of feeding last season's hay ensures that no vitamin A is present at all! Hay made during a period of adverse weather will contain still fewer nutrients and will require extensive supplementation. Examination of the data in Table 8.2 will also show that grass hay will

Table 8.1 Effect of method of conservation of grass on nutrient content

	Nutrient	Fresh grass	Dried grass	Grass hay
g per kg dry matter	Calcium	6.0	6.3	3.0
	Phosphorus	3.5	3.3	1.8
	Magnesium	1.7	2.1	1.0
	Sodium	1.9	1.7	1.0
mg per kg dry matter	Copper	8.0	8.0	3.2
	Cobalt	0.1	0.14	0.06
	Selenium	0.05	0.04	0.01
iu per kg dry matter	Vitamin A	30,000–200,000	30,000–150,000	2,000–5,000
	Vitamin D	-	-	340–1,600
	Vitamin E	100–300	100–250	4–20

be inadequate for pregnant and lactating mares, as well as the fact that it will be deficient in protein. However, it should contain virtually all the micronutrients required by the horse at rest without the need for supplementation.

It is relatively easy to cut large quantities of grass at any chosen stage of growth. The use of modern machinery allows the harvesting of forage from a large area in only a few hours, so there really is no excuse for herbage not to be harvested at the chosen stage of growth. Fig. 25 illustrates the different growth stages of grass from the young plant through to full flowering when the seeds are set, and the significance of stage of growth at harvest has already been mentioned in Chapter 7. In short, if you intend to produce hay you have to decide on the balance between yield and quality. Early-cut

grass is of high quality but low yield, whereas late-cut grass is of poor quality but high yield. If you are producing the hay for your own horses, obviously you will best know their requirements. Broodmares and foals will thrive on early cut hay, whereas late-cut hay may be more suitable for mature, unworked horses. For most people the best compromise is to cut grass when the ear/seedhead is first emerging; legumes should be cut at the pre-bloom stage.

Conservation of Grass

by:

Curing	=	Hay
Ensiling	=	Silage
Dehydration	=	Dried grass

Table 8.2 Percentage of required nutrients supplied to a 200kg (up to 12.2hh) pony and a 500kg horse fed only hay

200kg pony fed 4kg hay dry matter

Status of Animal	Energy %	Protein %	Calcium %	Phosphorus %
Rest	84–110	61–115	205	153
Late pregnancy	74–97	49–92	103	77
Moderate work	56–73	41–77	117	92
Early lactation	45–59	26–49	61	51

500kg horse fed 10kg hay dry matter

Status of Animal	Energy %	Protein %	Calcium %	Phosphorus %
Rest	116–152	69–130	205	164
Late pregnancy	103–135	55–104	117	85
Moderate work	77–101	46–86	137	110
Early lactation	68–88	32–60	73	64

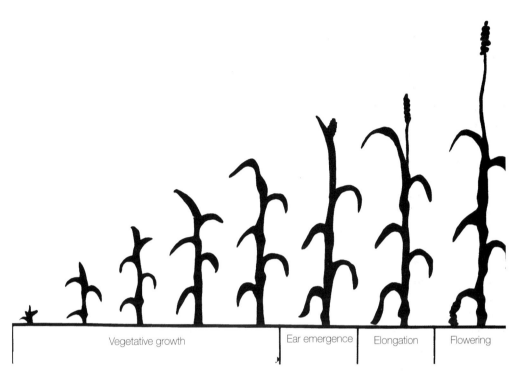

Fig 25 The stages of grass growth.

The digestibility of grass is affected by leaf-to-stem ratios. In very young grass the stem is more digestible than the leaf, but with advancing maturity the digestibility of the leaf decreases only very slowly, whereas the stem's digestibility declines rapidly. There is an increase in fibre content from below 20 per cent of the dry matter in young grass to as much as 40 per cent in the mature crop (*see* Fig 23, Chapter 7). As the figure shows, the stem comprises an increasing proportion of the herbage and thus exerts a much greater influence on the digestibility of the whole plant. It is therefore imperative that in any conservation process leaf loss is minimized as the leaf is both nutrient rich and digestible.

Hay

This has been the traditional means of conserving grass in the United Kingdom and some owners find it impossible to consider an alternative, even though they may be aware that generally it has a poor feed value. Unfortunately it is often the case that owners regard their hay as being of high quality, when in fact laboratory analysis would indicate that it was of very low nutritional value. The problem is that many people judge the quality of their hay on the basis of it being sweet-smelling and green in colour, and free from mould and dust. While these criteria are perfectly valid and obviously you would not want the reverse, they are still not enough. In order to judge the nutritional value of hay you need to go on to consider the stage of growth of the grass when cut. A broad guide is that if you can recognize seedheads, then the material will be of low nutritional value, although species is also important and a ryegrass-dominated hay would be of better feed value than, say, timothy hay. So before buying any large quantity of hay it would be sensible to have a sample analysed in order to obtain some objective idea of feed value.

To summarize, the two most important factors with regard to hay quality in the United Kingdom are:

- The age of the grass when it was cut. Traditionally it is always cut when it is mature, and no doubt part of the reason for this is that the UK climate is so unreliable; in addition, hay is made much more quickly if the grass is mature, as it is already drier when cut. Thus following this policy, the material is of poor quality to start with.
- The success of the hay-making operation itself. Changeable weather during the making process will involve repeated handling of the crop with resultant loss of leaf. Also, the baling of inadequately dried material means that there will be sufficient water to support the growth of moulds.

Unfortunately therefore, most hay made in the UK, or in countries with a similar climate, is mature, stemmy and of low quality. This is regrettable because horses fed solely on such hay will almost certainly be protein deficient, and most likely calcium deficient as well. It is generally thought that hay contains calcium in adequate amounts and in the correct ratio with phosphorus (*see* pages 75–6); however, recent studies have clearly shown that this is not the case. Horses that rely totally on hay for their nutrient supply may in fact be seriously deficient in some key nutrients.

It is owed purely to climatic conditions that very little legume hay is made in the United Kingdom, which is somewhat unfortunate because it is usually of better quality than grass hay. Legume leaves dry out very quickly because they are thin with a large surface area, whereas the stems are very thick and slow to dry. The result of this difference in drying rates between stem and leaf is that in the UK where the drying rate is generally slow anyway there are usually substantial leaf losses, and in extreme circumstances the end result can be a very stemmy hay of low feed value; plainly such poor quality samples are to be avoided. This tendency towards leaf loss means that legume hays produced in the UK can be very dusty when fed to horses and they are also more susceptible to mould growth because the stems are inadequately dried. Clearly then, while grass hay is disadvantaged as regards nutritional value when compared with legume hay, a dust- and mould-free sample may still be preferable.

Substantial quantities of alfalfa hay are imported into the UK from the USA and Canada at considerable expense, so this material is normally double-pressed to increase density and thus reduce shipping costs. However, while field drying in these countries is usually quite rapid, leaf shatter can still be a problem – so legume hays are not an 'ideal' alternative to hay.

Selecting Hays

Roughages can provide nutrients to keep the horse alive; indigestible fibre to maintain gut function; occupational therapy (keeping the horse occupied) to ensure normal behaviour – and spores and dust to impair respiratory function – oops!

Roughage is a vital component of the horse or pony diet. It can be good for him, bad for him, or even a combination of the two when it provides both nutrients and mould spores. Horses are mostly kept for their athletic ability, so the primary consideration has to be to feed clean, dust- and mould-free roughages. Thus, roughages should be purchased on this basis alone, since nutrients can be obtained by the sensible use of other mould-free foodstuffs. Conventional roughages vary in quality from very good to atrocious, so you need to ensure you only buy clean samples if you are reliant on grass hay for your horse.

In order to minimize the risk of buying contaminated hay you should be guided by your basic senses of sight, smell and touch. If it is green in colour, this indicates that it has been made very quickly. The best examples of this are artificially dehydrated crops such as grass or alfalfa which retain all their green colour. The longer grass lies in the field, the more pigment (chlorophyll) is lost due to the effects of light (a process known as photo-oxidation). Grass hay which is beige to brown in colour has therefore been in the field a long time and probably been repeatedly 'handled' by machinery with the inevitable loss of nutritive leaf. Furthermore, exposure of drying grass to rain will result in the loss of soluble nutrients from the partly dried crop; the presence of moisture also supports the growth of field fungi with resultant spore production. In optimum conditions, sun and wind combine to dry a grass crop very quickly, so that a minimum of machinery handling is required; under these conditions the green colour is retained. Provided the grass hay contains less than 20 per cent moisture (and preferably less than 14 per cent) then there will be insufficient water to support mould growth.

In order to assess hay when you go to buy it, follow these practical guidelines:

1. Assess the colour: the greener the better, provided of course that the hay is properly dried.
2. Assess the smell: it should appear fresh, often sweet-smelling and never musty or 'fusty'. If you are inexperienced you can learn to judge 'smell' by regularly assessing different quality hays.
3. 'Nose' the hay: an activity closely related to wine tasting no doubt! By carefully nosing each sample it will soon be obvious which hays are clean and 'well made', and which are not. Avoid inhaling deeply, since mould spores and dust are not good for *your* lungs, either.
4. Touch the hay to assess obvious dampness. Handling it will also enable you to assess dustiness and the extent of mould contamination.
5. Shake it out. By shaking out hay in shafts of light you will be able to see dust and mould particles. However, remember that no hay is completely dust-free unless dust has been mechan-

ically extracted, so confirmation of actual spore content should be provided by specialist laboratory services.

6. Scrunching hay in your hands will immediately inform you if it is soft or spiky. The latter feeling indicates mature stemmy grass, which is more likely to have achieved the appropriate level of dryness because it would have been drier at the outset. Soft grass hay is made from immature grass, contains more water, and takes longer to dry out satisfactorily. Again, information on the water content and spore count can be provided by a laboratory, but often this takes time and purchasing decisions may have to be taken quickly. However, skilled use of the senses together with common sense should help you to make the right decision.

So far there has been much talk of laboratory analysis. Just what can this tell us? In addition to providing detailed information on the water content and spore count, laboratory analysis can give you the protein, fibre and mineral content of the hay. The significance of these findings will depend upon the role that the hay is to play in the ration of your horses. Where the ration is totally hay-based the protein content is crucially important, but where hay provides only 30 per cent of the ration it is obviously far less so. A 500kg (10cwt) horse fed to maintenance and receiving 10kg (22lb) of hay per day might receive anything between 400g and 800g (15oz and 1lb 12oz) of protein daily, depending on whether the hay is of poor quality (4 per cent protein), or good quality (8 per cent protein). Thus the protein

supply might vary from grossly inadequate to acceptable, and it is apparent that feeding poor hay will significantly disadvantage the horse. However, if the same horse were fed only 30 per cent of the ration as hay (3kg/6lb 10oz), the protein supplied could vary between 120 and 240g a day and would not have such a large impact on the horse's protein supply (assuming the concentrate contained sufficient protein).

Alternatives to Hay

Owing to the number of variables involved in making and selecting good quality hay, it is no wonder that many people are now looking for convenient, superior alternatives. In addition, farmers are turning away from the conventional production of hay, so less is generally available than before. So what are the options?

Grass can be conserved in ways other than the traditional field-curing process. Some rely on the process of dehydration, while others depend upon a 'pickling' process of preservation.

Barn-dried hay This is made from grass that is partly dried on the field, but which is then baled, and put into a barn where air is blown through the stack to complete the drying process. The advantage of this hay over traditional hay is hygienic quality. This way of making hay is less dependent on good weather because the grass is baled whilst still quite wet, and there is minimal leaf loss due to minimal handling. Exposure to sunlight is reduced, so barn-dried hay is characteristically very green, leafy, dust-free and of good hygienic quality.

Field-cured forage stored outside is at risk of nutrient loss.

Consequently it commands a high price, although its nutritive value may not be very different from field-dried hay since both are largely dependent for their feed value on the stage of growth at which they are cut. Thus, barn-dried hay may be extremely 'clean' but if it is made from mature grass, its nutritive value cannot be high.

Dried grass The production of this material depends upon dehydrating the grass by artificial means alone. Thus the crop is cut in the field, chopped, and then transported to a large drying machine fired by coal, gas or oil where it is dried at temperatures up to 800°C. You might think these high temperatures to be destructive, but because the grass is exposed to them for only a few seconds they are not. It needs only to be heated long enough to drive off the water, and it is then cooled. The grass is not fully dessicated, so 5 to 10 per cent water remains, which has a protective effect in that the grass itself never 'cooks' and so does not lose nutrients. The resultant 'hay' is green and dust-free, and until now it has been ground and pelleted. Dried grass pellets are very variable in quality, which as with other 'hays' depends upon the type and age of grass used as the raw material. Now very high-quality, long-chop dried grass is available, which is an excellent alternative to hay.

Hydroponic grass This is grass grown in a unit within the stable yard. Although it can

Hydroponic grass in a large unit, producing 1,000kg (20cwt) a day.

Section through trays of hydroponically growing grass, and showing six days' growth: the youngest bottom left, the oldest top right.

be of high quality, it can never be a total replacement for other roughage in the diet, unless a large machine is purchased.

Bagged grass products There are various types of bagged grass product, each of which is produced using a slightly different method. Examples are:

Haylage: This is made from wilted grass baled when the moisture content is around 45 per cent. The bales are then compressed to half their size and sealed into plastic bags where anaerobic (without air) fermentation can progress until a steady state is achieved. This is exactly the same process used to make big bale silage. Haylage was originally made just from grasses, but realizing that the horse-owning public appreciated the feed value of legumes such as alfalfa, Haylage based on both alfalfa and sainfoin is now produced. These products are excellent for horses with respiratory problems but they have two major disadvantages. First, once the bag is opened, or if it is damaged, the contents must be used up straightaway as secondary fermentation occurs; and second, it tends to be expensive as approximately half a bag's content is water. However, horses do like it as its texture is far more like grass than hay.

Hay-based products: Hay produced in the conventional way, but then processed after storage through a cleaner. The process does remove dust, spores and soil contaminants, but it may also remove a lot of the nutritious leafy material. Once cleaned, boiling molasses are added and it is then sealed in a bag under pressure. As it is made in the conventional way at first,

its nutritive value will be governed by the same factors as field-cured hay.

Grass silage: A conserved grass product made by controlled fermentation either in a clamp, a silage tower or a big bale; or more simply 'pickled' grass. For silage-making the grass is cut much younger than for hay, at the ear-emergence stage, so the starting material is of much higher quality. The conservation or making process should result in little loss, although good quality silage is only made if the system is air-tight and is acidic. This is easier to achieve in clamps or towers, but big bales are more vulnerable to damage, and if air is able to enter it can unacceptably change the fermentation pattern.

Silage may be fed to horses as the sole roughage, and horse owners living near a farm may benefit from the use of clamp or tower silage. For others, it is perfectly possible to obtain and feed big bale silage. However, horses have died following the consumption of contaminated big bale silage so users must be particularly careful to discard bales whose outer covering has been damaged, or when the contents are not acid (indicated by an

Replacement rates for 1kg of hay	
Fresh young grass	2.45kg
Fresh mature grass	2.75kg
Dried grass	0.64kg
Clamp silage	2.04kg
Big-bale silage	1.97kg

Chemically treated straw in big bales.

unpleasant ammoniacal smell). Silage is another useful forage for those horses suffering from COPD.

Straw-based roughages These cannot be considered as alternatives to hay for feeding to horses, since they contain too much indigestible fibre. Their main role is as non-nutritive bulk, which can be used to slow the rate of consumption of hard feed and to satisfy appetite. They are usually dust-free because they are heavily molassed, a component which can itself represent a useful source of energy to the horse, although on a cost per unit of energy they are generally very expensive compared to other products.

Herb-based chaffs: Some are made from chopped wheat straw with limestone, herbs and molasses added. While it will provide hours of enjoyable chewing, it is of minimal nutritive value.

Other products are made from short chopped straw, but the type is not declared. These may contain molasses and herb extracts and claim to be equivalent in feed value to hay, although as we know this can range from very poor to very good! They contain about 10 per cent sugar and so must contain a lot of molasses. On an as-fed basis, they are probably equivalent to hays of low protein content, although they should be free from respirable particles that could affect lung function.

Chops: Based on the feeding straws, barley and oats, these contain some hay although the proportions are not stated. In addition, salt, limestone, seaweed and molasses are added; the latter must be present in quite large quantities since the total sugar content is declared at 17½ per cent and the fibre is only 19 per cent. However, other nutrients are not declared in the literature, so one is left guessing about protein and energy values.

Chaffs: A blend of straw and molasses, of which variants are available that either contain herbs or have vitamins and minerals added. These high fibre products are of low nutritive value and all have a very similar low protein and energy content.

Alfalfa-based roughages Dried alfalfa is produced in the UK by harvesting at a pre-determined stage of growth (pre-bloom stage). The material is cut in the field and wilted for a few hours before being picked up by a forage harvester which precision-chops it. It is conveyed to the drying plant where it is dried at the rate of 6+ tonnes per hour, cooled and then packaged. Thus the conservation process is completed within a day, and because the alfalfa is always cut at the same stage of growth it has a uniform composition: 16 per cent protein and a digestible energy content of between 9 and 10 MJ per kilogram.

The conservation losses are minimal and because the alfalfa is heat-treated, bacterial and mould contaminants which are present on all herbage, are rendered non-viable. Molasses is added after drying to trap any leaf particles, and the low water content of the final product is inadequate to support the growth of fungi during storage. Thus the material has a very long shelf-life and does not require preservative. Dried alfalfa is available in three major forms:

Alfalfa pellets: Dried alfalfa is ground, molassed and then pelleted. They are available in different sizes (4, 6 and 8mm) and are normally declared to contain 16 per cent protein. Imported alfalfa pellets can be purchased which contain different levels of protein. The major disadvantage of all these alfalfa pellets is that they provide little occupational therapy, even though they are fibrous forage!

Chopped alfalfa: This is high quality alfalfa that has been precision-chopped (2–4cm/¾–1½in) and then dried quickly; 5 per cent molasses is then added to bind the leaf and to keep the product dust-free. It is high in protein and energy, and like all alfalfa products is a very good natural source of vitamins and minerals. In common with other chops, horses have to bite more often to consume it, and mouthfuls are generally smaller compared to those taken by horses fed the more conventional 'long' roughages.

Alfalfa/straw blends: A 50:50 mix of molassed alfalfa and molassed conservation grade oat straw that has been precision-chopped. Although oat straw has always been considered to be the best feeding straw, its nutrient contribution is fairly small and the analysis provided largely reflects that of the alfalfa component. Many owners fail to appreciate that in fact that the total protein content is a meaningless figure because what is important to the horse is how much protein he can digest. Generally, all straw proteins are poorly digested by horses.

Comparison between Roughages

Higher dry matter products such as Super Molichop contain more nutrients per kilo than low dry matter products such as hydroponic grass. Generally, the lower the dry matter, the more the horse or pony will have to eat to obtain the nutrents that he needs. Straw-based roughages are generally very fibrous and of low nutritive value compared to those based on alfalfa which are of high quality; bagged grass products occupy an intermediate position. All of these products are very good for feeding to horses and ponies that are known to be allergic to spores and dust.

Straw-based roughages and bagged grass products are costly sources of energy, and the former in particular are very expensive, especially as they could never be considered as hay-replacers. Alfalfa products are the cheapest source of

protein and hay is the cheapest source of energy.

ENERGY CONCENTRATES

Cereals

Generally, cereals are very good energy sources. They contain about 10 per cent protein but are deficient in calcium, having calcium/phosphorus ratio between 1:4 and 1:8. To achieve an ideal 2:1 ratio of these minerals, limestone will need to be added to the diet. Where cereals are mixed 50:50 with forage as for horses in hard work, then the overall protein may be quite low if poor quality hay is used and protein supplements would be required. Another feature of cereals is that most of the energy is stored as starch, and as mentioned in Chapter 3, the horse is not well equipped to deal with this material. Large meals of cereal and sudden large changes in intake can cause an oversupply of starch which may pass through the stomach and small intestine undigested to be fermented in the hind

Examples of cereals fed to horses. From left: maize; oats; wheat; barley; naked oats.

gut with disastrous consequences for the horse. Thus cereals by themselves are concentrated sources of energy which require supplementation and must be fed carefully.

Oats

Oats are generally regarded as the most important cereal for working horses. It has been shown that of the cereals, horses prefer oats. Although it is considered inadvisable to feed freshly harvested oats, there is no evidence for this. Oats are less digestible than cereals such as barley and maize because of their high fibre content; this fibre makes oats a less concentrated feed than other cereals, and therefore somewhat 'safer' to use in the hands of the inexperienced owner. A common mistake is to feed other cereals in place of oats on the basis of equal volume – the same number of scoops, for example. But it is imperative that feeds are substituted on the basis of *weight* and their energy content, otherwise overfeeding will result when oats are replaced.

Oats demonstrate great variation in their fibre content and subsequently their feed value and this variation can have quite a large effect on their nutrient content. For example, protein can vary between 8 and 13 per cent and digestible energy between 11 and 14 MJ. When assessing oats, ensure they are plump, shiny, clean and dust-free; grains that are elongated and thin contain a lot of husk and are of low feed value.

Naked oats are a fairly recently developed alternative to the traditional oat. They are simply 'husk-less' oats, and because the husk is the major source of variability, the levels of nutrients present in the grain and in particular the oil content are greatly improved. The benefit is that the horse can become less dependent on starch-rich concentrates because overall concentrate feeding levels may be reduced. Those performance horses with poor appetite can more easily meet their energy requirements from naked oats. It is quite possible that the traditional oat could be replaced by naked oats as the major energy source for racehorses and performance horses.

Barley

Barley is being increasingly used because of the expense of using traditional oats, and because of its less variable composition. Micronized, flaked barley is very popular as an ingredient of coarse mixes and is also useful by itself. It has always been recognized that barley is more energy-dense than oats due to its lower fibre content, and it has the reputation of being fattening! However, all foods are fattening when fed to excess! Horses that were not 'doing' or were 'under the weather' were often fed boiled barley as it was recognized to be a very good source of digestible energy. Micronized or extruded barley fulfils the same function, with the advantage of removing the laborious boiling process. Micronized flaked barley is a very attractive product, being of breakfast cereal quality and thus very palatable. In feed quality it approaches that of naked oats, although the high oil content of the latter ensures a higher energy content. While barley grains are denser than husked oats, the micronized product is not and this serves to emphasize how important it is to *weigh* the feed and to substitute feeds on the basis of energy value expressed per kg of product. The importance of lower density, cooked products such as micronized or extruded barley is that they take longer for the horse or pony to consume, and with improved digestibility they are less likely to lead to a starch overload in the hind gut.

Used correctly, barley is an excellent source of concentrated energy but because, in its raw form, it is generally harder than oats, it is best rolled prior to feeding.

Maize

Maize is the most energy-dense of the conventional cereals because it has the lowest fibre and highest oil content. It can be fed whole to horses, although most of the time in the UK it is processed and fed as flaked maize. This is produced by steam-treating the grains and then hot-rolling them. The product is recognized as a highly palatable, energy-rich feed which is usually only fed to those animals that need to be tempted to eat, or those with very high energy requirements. The process partially dextrinizes the starch, thereby making the product more digestible.

Bran

Bran is, the best known by-product of flour production. It has been fed to horses for decades, and has been the cause of bone disease. It is also well known for its imbalance of calcium and phosphorus (1:8); otherwise it is a good source of protein. However, its cost exceeds its nutritional worth, and its inclusion in horse diets for its contribution of fibre cannot be justified. Its continued use

by so many owners is a tribute to the persistence of traditional practices!

Oil

Any vegetable oil can be fed to boost the energy intake of horses, but it is important to remember that these oils are rich in polyunsaturated fats so that not only are they liable to go rancid, but they will also increase the horse's requirement for vitamin E. In terms of quantity, many horse owners feed very little oil, often giving only a cupful per day. Horses appear to digest oil very well, however, and have been fed in excess of 1kg (2lb) per day when in work. Thus it appears that oil can be safely fed in horse diets as an alternative energy source. Furthermore, there is work to suggest that it is positively beneficial in the diets of endurance horses, where the indications are that the horse adapts biochemically to using fat/oil as an energy substitute, removing the dependency on glucose. This has the effect of delaying the onset of fatigue.

Another aspect of oil use is that of using mixtures of fish and vegetable oils. Not only can the oils represent an energy source, they also provide essential fatty acids, one of which (EPA) has beneficial effects in both arthritic and skin conditions.

PROTEIN CONCENTRATES

Linseed

This has long been the favourite of the traditional horse keeper. Boiling linseed is necessary to destroy poisons contained within the seed, and at the same time the indigestible mucilage contained within the seeds is liberated. This absorbs a lot of water and produces the characteristic jelly which, when fed, lubricates the bowel. The oil present can improve coat condition in those horses fed indifferent diets. However, there are much better protein sources available to the horse owner who wishes to produce his/her own feed mixtures.

Soya Bean

Toasted soya is available either fat-extracted, or as full-fat soya containing up to 20 per cent fat. This latter product is more expensive and is often contained in coarse mixes where it provides both energy and protein. Most extracted forms of soya contain about 44 per cent protein which is usually of such good quality that soya can be the sole protein source in diets for horses. It provides lysine, which is the essential amino acid that is vital for good growth.

White Fishmeal

This is probably the best source of dietary protein for animals, but it is expensive and its use is generally restricted to creep feeds for foals, although it may be incorporated into compound feeds for horses. Few owners buy fishmeal because it not always readily available from feed merchants.

Peas and Beans

Beans are usually cracked before feeding to horses, and field peas are micronized and flaked. Nowadays, peas are probably more popular for feeding to horses than beans. They both contain about 24 per cent protein and are particularly potent sources of lysine. Peas are very palatable and are thus a very useful ingredient in horse diets.

More detailed guidance on how to balance feed ingredients to produce a diet is given in Chapters 10, 11 and 13.

Summary Points

- By carefully considering both the nutrient content and the cost of supplying nutrients in different roughages, it is possible to minimize the day-to-day costs of feeding.
- Of the non-compound concentrates, the horse owner has a modest number of energy and protein sources to select from.
- In most cases the first choice cereal will be oats, although barley is cheaper and a better energy source.
- Of the protein sources, soya is the best choice, with perhaps some 'processed' (micronized) peas.
- Simple mixtures of these materials would be calcium deficient (easily rectified by the addition of limestone); vitamin additions would depend on the circumstance of the horse's feeding.

9

COMPOUND
FEEDS

Compound feeds are commercially produced mixtures of selected raw materials which are blended together by various processes to achieve a desired nutrient content; most have been processed in some way or another. Traditionally the raw materials include cereals, protein sources and by-products, and these are proportioned, mixed and milled together to form a 'grist', a fine particulate mixture of ingredients (*see* page 92). To this is added the premixtures of mineral and vitamins necessary to obtain the desired levels of these nutrients. Originally horse compounds were only available as cubes and the range on offer was fairly limited, with only general horse and pony, stud and performance products. Muesli-like coarse mixes were then introduced, and immediately the product range doubled.

Knowing which product to feed can cause a lot of frustration. It might seem easy: obviously a foal creep feed is for a foal; yet when you add to this a range which includes rearing diet, yearling cubes, breeding mixes and so on, the picture becomes far more complicated. What follows is an explanation of the meanings of various labels on compound feeds, including what the products are and the implications of their use in practice.

LABELLING

By law, feed manufactures must attach to a bag of their product a label which can then be used to identify the manufacturer, the place of manufacture and the batch number of the feed. Thus in the unlikely event of a purchaser wishing to complain about the product they can do so directly; and in a case of complaint, the manufacturer always requires the purchaser to return the appropriate bag label so that the batch of feed in question can be identified. This is particularly important if a serious error in manufacture has occurred, and a whole batch of feed has been contaminated. Fortunately this is extremely rare in practice because horse feed manufacturers take great care and institute stringent control procedures.

It is further required that the percentages of protein, fibre, ash and oil are declared on the bag label, although in most cases these figures mean very little to the purchaser, apart perhaps from protein. Due to the variation between different lorry loads of cereal from all over the country and those that are imported, the manufacturer is allowed some leeway on the values he prints on the label. While he may decide on a finished feed specification of 10 per cent protein, it is impossible to be totally accurate, so the actual value may be above or below this figure, although there are limits to the amount of variation that is allowed.

For nutritionally beneficial nutrients such as protein and oil there is very little leeway under the declaration, while an excess is much more acceptable. In contrast, there are tight upper limits on both fibre and ash, because too much fibre has adverse effects on the horse's ability to use the food, and ash contains no energy. For these two nutrients it is generally thought that the lower the level, the better, and thus the manufacturer has wide lower limits; whereas for both protein and oil he must be very careful not to undersupply. In general, low ash feeds are high in energy, and low fibre feeds are more digestible. Thus high performance feeds should be low in ash and fibre, and possibly high in oil. It then follows that maintenance cubes will be high in fibre (and possibly also ash) and low in oil and protein. The result of all this 'allowed' legal variation is that you could be feeding your horse or pony more or less than you think.

If vitamins are added during manufacture, this will be stated on the label as 'vitamin levels are guaranteed until...' or 'vitamins present until...'. In order that the stated levels of vitamin activity can be guaranteed until a certain date, extra vitamins are added at manufacture; these 'overages' are carefully calculated on the basis of known decay rates. This means that a bag of feed will contain more of a vitamin when it is initially purchased, so that it can maintain the guaranteed levels until the 'expiry' date stated on the label.

A recent innovation is the listing of raw materials, probably reflecting the public interest in food labelling. Cubes may be composed of cheap by-products, and inclusion of whole cereal may be low. It is impossible for the layperson to identify the raw material of cubed diets, and thus manufacturers can employ their skills to utilize all sorts of raw materials that the average horse feeder might consider unsuitable and would certainly never see or dream of feeding to a favourite horse or pony. However, manufacturers compounded feeds for competition horses employ rigorous quality controls and only use the best quality materials; some have feed mills solely dedicated to the production of horse feed.

There has always been an innate suspicion of cubes amongst horse owners, and the advent of the coarse mix largely set their minds at rest since in most cases individual ingredients are easily recognized. However, ground materials are still included, often in a 3mm pellet that also contains the vitamin/mineral premix. There is a tendency towards using fairly heavy applications of syrups or mollassed-based by-products to prevent any dustiness. Obviously, horses with their 'sweet tooth' are attracted towards this type of product and generally the products are very palatable. The generous use of these sweeteners prevents the horse from selecting out or separating less palatable ingredients, so that the owners are basically well-pleased with the horse's response to coarse mixes.

All bags of compound feed come with feeding guidelines enabling you to decide how much your horse may require. You should remember that these are already 'balanced' feeds: that is, they contain everything your horse needs without additions. If you do not stick to these guidelines, perhaps because you want to add a little sugar beet to the ration for instance, you will unbalance the diet.

TYPES OF PRODUCT

There are cubes or coarse mixes available to meet most conceivable needs and each manufacturer normally produces a complete range of products, from stud cubes to performance mixes. Nowadays there are also some special-purpose products available, such as balancers which are used to

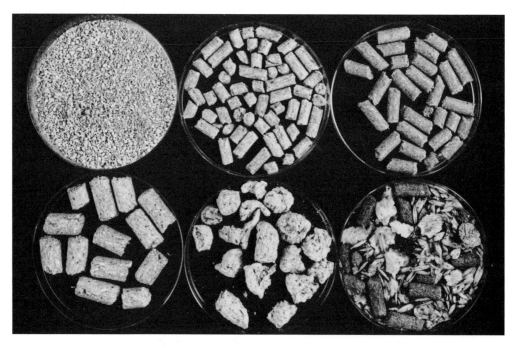

Examples of compound feeds. Clockwise from top left: Grist; 6mm pellets; 8mm pellets; Coarse mix; Extruded feed; 12mm pellets.

supplement the diets of performance horses that are still fed on traditional 'straight' cereals. A more recent addition to 'special-purpose' feeds is the very high energy premix designed to be fed in small quantities to horses in hard work, such as endurance horses who can benefit from supplementary fat. What follows is a description of the more usual compound feeds currently in use.

Cubes

These are made by forcing the mixture of ingredients through a die under pressure. Cubes can be different sizes, ranging from 12, 10, 8, 6, 4 and 3mm in size. The most popular are 6 and 8mm. Small pellets seem to take longer to eat, and greedy feeders (particularly hungry ponies) seem less likely to choke on the smaller size. Small pellets are often incorporated as part of coarse mixes to supply protein, vitamins and minerals.

The ingredients used to form a cube must remain bound together and this is achieved in a number of different ways:
1. The physical pressure exerted in forcing the ingredients through a die can be sufficient to stick them together.
2. Steam can be added, and this also has a partial cooking effect.
3. Binders may be added; molasses is quite popular for this purpose, although numerous other substances are available.

Coarse mixes

Coarse mixes contain cereals which have themselves been processed, usually by micronizing. Flaking and rolling ingredients is also common practice. Coarse mixes containing uncooked materials treated in this way should be used quickly or they will decline in freshness. Quite high levels of molasses and/or other sugar-rich additives may be used, and these are vulnerable to deterioration because they contain a lot of water. Consequently, preservatives such as proprionic acid may be added to inhibit fungal growths. Another ingredient often used in coarse mixes is dried alfalfa. This is processed first by drying, and then with the addition of a little molasses it is made into 6mm pellets. This product is similar to the dried grass in that it has the qualities of a concentrate, is produced from only fresh forage, and is a complete feed in itself.

Extruded Products

Extrusion is a technology which has recently been applied to horse feeds, although the technique has been used for quite a long time in the production of cereal-based dog feeds. Raw starch which is present in untreated cereals can be substantially affected by the extrusion process: this increases the temperature of the feed, resulting in the breakdown of starch thus enabling easier digestion. It is possible to extrude a variety of feed mixtures in this way to make them more digestible. Extruded products have a low density and thus occupy a greater volume per kilogram compared to raw cereals. This is beneficial because they take longer to eat.

RAW MATERIALS

The better quality raw material such as full-fat soya and cereals can provide the basis for a premium product, necessary for hard-working horses or breeding stock. Quality control of these raw materials will affect the quality of the end product. Coarse mixes allow the owner the opportunity of examining the ingredients whereas it is impossible for the average person to determine exactly what has gone into producing a cube of extruded product – and the manufacturer is not obliged to tell us in detail!

There is a temptation to add new and unusual ingredients to improve product appeal. Herbs are frequently used and have lots of 'green' and 'health' appeal. Recently, of course, probiotics (*see* end of chapter), have made their way into horse feeds as well, and while it is unlikely that any of these 'new' additions will do harm, will they do any good, and are they really necessary? We desperately need some sound, objective feeding trial information on all these different feed ingredients so that we know their relative values in horse and pony diets.

SUPPLEMENTS

Supplements are bought because the horse owner wishes the best for his horse, is worried into using them, or wants to try something that will give him the competitive edge. By contrast, there are many who would never consider using a supplement at any time. Very often the use, misuse and avoidance of supplements is based on hearsay and prejudice rather than sound knowledge.

Traditionally supplements have been composed of mixtures of trace mineral, major mineral and vitamins mixed through a 'carrier', and these products were designed to be used on a daily basis in reasonably small doses. Recently we have seen the introduction of Macro supplements which also contain a lot of protein and are to be fed at a higher level. These latter products are probably more correctly described as 'balancers' since they provide the protein which may be lacking in the basal ration.

The component parts of a supplement may then be as follows:

Vitamins, which may include fat- and water-soluble vitamins.

Trace minerals, of which the most important are copper, iron, zinc, selenium, manganese, iodine and cobalt.

Amino acids: lysine is extremely important, with methionine the next, particularly as it is a source of organic sulphur.

Additives: there are a number of substances that can be incorporated within this grouping, such as Dimethylglycine (DMG), Methylsulphonylmethane (MSM), Carnitine and Yea Sacc. The latter is composed of viable cells and might therefore also be considered to be a probiotic (*see* last section).

Protein, of which soya is the most popular, although dried milk is often used and linseed may be included to appease the traditionalists.

The minerals and vitamins are usually mixed or dispersed through a carrier, so for example, although the daily dose of a supplement may be 50g (1.7oz) the active ingredients may only constitute 10g (0.3oz); the remaining 40g (1.4oz) is made up of a carrier, of which the simplest and cheapest is limestone which contains about 33 per cent calcium.

The purpose of the carrier is to separate micronutrients which are aggressive to one another; the nutrients are dispersed throughout it instead of being concentrated together. Another reason for using a carrier is to make the supplement more palatable; if it is then obviously this will improve the intake of the micronutrients which, in themselves, are often unpalatable. You should also be aware that the carrier that is used will in itself act as a source of nutrients.

Choosing a Suitable Supplement

The choice of supplement to use will depend upon a number of factors:
1. Nutrient specification.
2. Cost.
3. Effective doses.
4. Suitability for the type of horse.
In order to achieve a 'complete' ration by making up any shortfall in the diet, the complexity of the supplement must vary according to the circumstances in which it is fed. For example, a child's pony ridden infrequently and fed poor quality roughage will require a different type of supplement than the racehorse in full training fed good quality hay and oats. Thus it is worthwhile considering the effect of different feeding régimes on the micronutrient needs of horses.

The horse at grass The domestication of the horse and agricultural development have significantly affected the micronutrient intake of the grazing horse, and in some cases has created the need for a supplement.

Horses fed conserved grass Horses maintained on only hay and chop/chaff mixtures are likely to be deficient in a large number of nutrients. The incorporation of high levels of molasses in straw-based mixtures adds water which aids the deterioration of vitamins, and lysine and methionine will be low in the ration anyway, thus creating the need for a supplement.

Horses fed conserved grass together with concentrates The compounded feed is nutrient dense, and will contribute significantly to meeting the vitamin and mineral requirements of the horse. Most companies produce a range of feeds aimed at different sections of the market, stud cubes for example. They differ in nutrient content in an attempt to meet the needs of a particular group of horses, although they may fall short of meeting individual need. Furthermore, the level of compound fed will govern the proportion of micronutrient requirements that are met.

Oversupplementation

This may arise through overdosing: if one measure is good for the horse, then two measures are twice as good! Alternatively, the problem can arise through the use of different, non-complementary supplements. Different supplements are often used together because the owner is reluctant to place his faith in one product. If both are high in, say, the fat-soluble vitamins A and D, then it is possible that dangerously high levels may be achieved in the ration. Table 9.1 indicates the maximum tolerance levels for some of the minerals and vitamins.

Changes in horse-keeping practices, coupled with agricultural developments and advances in food processing technology, all mean that supplements are a way of guaranteeing that a horse obtains its correct vitamin and mineral intake. However, it is vital that the supplement is specifically tailored to the class of the horse being fed, and furthermore, the composition of the supplement should reflect sound scientific knowledge.

Horses are individuals and require individual feeding and care if they are to express their full potential; it is counterproductive to limit performance by undersupplying essential nutrients.

Probiotics

Probiotics are feed supplements which have a beneficial effect on the host animal by affecting the gut environment. The young foal quickly establishes a 'normal' gut flora which is a complex collection of numerous micro-organisms consisting of about 400 different types of bacteria. This flora is normally very stable, but it can be influenced by dietary and environmental factors, which can include:

- Excessive hygiene
- Antibiotic therapy
- Stress

Probiotics work in three main ways:

1. Antagonistic effects: by competing with pathogens (agents that cause disease) for available nutrients they disadvantage them.
2. Metabolic effects: by decreasing the activity of some enzymes they may increase the activity of more useful enzymes.

Table 9.1 Suggested maximum tolerance levels in the dietary dry matter (DM)

Trace minerals (mg per kg DM)	
Iron	1,000
Copper	800
Zinc	500
Selenium	2
Iodine	5
Fat-soluble vitamins (iu per kg DM)	
A	16,000
D	2,200
E	1,000

---

3. Stimulation of immunity: by increasing antibody levels and by stimulating activity of phagocytes (cells which engulf and consume foreign particles). Phagocytes are in essence killer cells that protect the body.

In an ideal situation, probiotics have little effect because they are most beneficial when there is some disruption of hindgut function. Obviously, probiotics should contain organisms that are capable of exerting a beneficial effect through colonizing the gut.

Summary Points

- Considerable technological development has gone into the production of the modern compound feed for horses; to take full advantage of this knowledge requires adherence to the manufacturer's recommendations.
- In practice, horse owners like to feed a variety of products and this tends to unbalance the overall diet, although rarely with dire consequences.
- Commercial hype seems to replace objective evaluation when it comes to promoting horse products. Notwithstanding this, commercially produced compound feeds have significant advantages:
  1. Convenience, as only one product needs to be purchased and fed in addition to roughage;
  2. Ingredients are checked for quality and balanced for the type of horse for which the feed is recommended and the necessary vitamins and minerals added;
  3. Cooking during processing should increase the digestibility of the food, and high temperatures will have a sterilizing effect on ingredients.
- The average horse owner will have to identify supplements that are suited to the individual horse's activity and then compare the nutrients supplied at the recommended dose rate in each manufacturer's product.
- Check that there is an effective quantity of the appropriate nutrients and then finally do the cost comparisons on a daily basis.
- If in doubt, seek expert advice!
- The micro-organisms present in the gut of horses are effective in providing resistance to disease.
- The composition of this protective flora can be altered by environmental changes which are stressful, such as dietary change. This can render the horse more susceptible to disease and/or reduce the efficiency of food breakdown.
- Probiotics may be used to redress the intestinal balance of micro-organisms and thereby ensure normality.
- It is important to realize that in many cases the consumption of probiotic by the horse will have no 'apparent' effect.

10

FEEDING FOR MAINTENANCE

Most horses and ponies spend the summer months out at grass, when providing the supply of grass is good and plentiful, they have the opportunity to build up reserves for the coming winter. Each day a horse can eat in excess of 10 per cent of his own bodyweight in fresh grass, and this grass will certainly provide all the nutrients required to maintain him and usually far more than he needs (*see* Table 10.1 for a comparison of grass products). There will be an excess of protein, for example, which will be broken down and used as an energy source as needed, or stored as fat for later use. Similarly, any surplus food energy will be stored in the same way. This

Table 10.1 Nutritive values

Feed	Dry matter (g per kg)	Composition of dry matter (g per kg)		
		DE (MJ)	Fibre	Protein
Fresh young grass	200	14.0	202	170
Fresh mature grass	250	10.0	310	87
Dried grass	900	12.0	204	180
Grass hay*	860	8.0	320	75
Clamp silage*	260	13.0	266	160
Big bale silage*	350	10.0	300	110

(* These products are very variable in their nutrient content: the figures are meant as a guide.)

is reflected in the horse's size: the more surplus food energy, the fatter he gets.

Horses turned out full time in the summer frequently get too fat, particularly if they are not worked. However, these stores of fat are beneficial in providing a back-up to compensate for inadequate winter feeding, especially where horses are wintered out. Free-ranging horses, such as New Forest ponies in the UK, rely on these times of plentiful food to build up reserves to help them over the winter when food resources are scarce and usually of poor quality.

Grass is a very good source of ß-carotene (from which vitamin A is formed), so summer grazing also enables the horse to establish reserves of vitamin A. Exposure to sunlight while at grass will also enable the horse to build a store of vitamin D. So good summer grazing and plenty of sunshine are a boon to horses which are likely to be wintered outdoors.

However, growing conditions are not always ideal during the summer and adverse weather may affect the rate of growth and the quality of grazing. Dry, hot weather curtails grass growth and where pastures have been severely droughted, most owners revert to feeding hay long before the onset of the cold weather. Consequently, many horses may enter the winter feeding period without the 'normal' body stores.

ENVIRONMENTAL EFFECTS ON ENERGY NEEDS

Horses that live out of doors in the wintertime are subjected to the rigours of the weather, and this can have a marked effect on their energy requirements. In a cold environment, horses will lose heat; to help combat this heat loss New Zealand rugs and field shelters should be provided, and extra feed should be given as well. The circumstances leading to heat loss, and the effects of the protective measures taken against them, have been measured to predict the horse's change in energy needs over the winter period. A summary of the results are shown in Table 10.2, and give an indication of the proportion of extra feed that is required. This table clearly shows that smaller horses are much more susceptible to bad weather and require more care with their feeding than do larger horses.

As mentioned above, the use of a New Zealand rug is to be recommended in terms of making the horse more comfortable and reducing the feed bills; the colder he is the more food he needs to produce heat, so it makes sense to prevent heat loss in the first place. Open-fronted field shelters do not seem to be as effective as rugs, although they are obviously beneficial. In most winters, both weather protection and additional feeding are required to prevent the horse losing condition, unless it is a heavy horse type.

A 500kg (10cwt) horse would normally need to consume about 9kg (20lb) of hay to maintain itself. In the absence of a shelter or rug, it would have to be fed an additional 1.5, 2.5 or 3.4kg (3.5, 5.8 or 8.5lb) of hay per day depending on whether it was a mild, average or harsh winter respectively. Thus an average winter would require the feeding of an additional bale of hay each week which would, of course, involve extra expense.

Table 10.2 The proportion of extra feed required (as a percentage of maintenance) by outwintered animals of different weights given different forms of weather protection

Liveweight (kg)	Protection	Type of winter		
		Mild	Average	Harsh
100		70	85	100
300	None	31	43	54
600		11	20	29
100		52	65	89
300	Open-fronted	20	31	41
600	shelter	4	11	20
100		35	47	59
300	N.Z. rug	9	18	28
600		0	4	10
100	N.Z. rug and	21	32	42
300	open-fronted	2	8	16
600	shelter	0	0	3

CHOICE OF FORAGE

The hay on offer for feeding over the winter is usually extremely variable in quality, and the choice of forage will be affected by a number of factors which we will examine.

Hygienic Quality

Hygienic quality is best judged by the presence, or absence, of mould and fungal spores. Although mouldy hay is recognized as a health hazard, the level of mould contamination is not always easy to judge; many owners fail to recognize mouldiness even though the dangers posed by it are well known. The extent to which mouldy hay is hazardous depends on the types and abundance of organisms present. The most critical factors determining mould development are water content and the presence or absence of heat; the greatest risk appears to come from roughages which have undergone a heating process. Thus:

• Hay baled at 15 to 20 per cent moisture heats very little and should be virtually dust-free. There will be some plant debris and pollen grains but if spores are present, they will be few. Perhaps surprisingly, the better hays have more non-spore dust than mouldy hays.

• Baling hay with a moisture content of 20

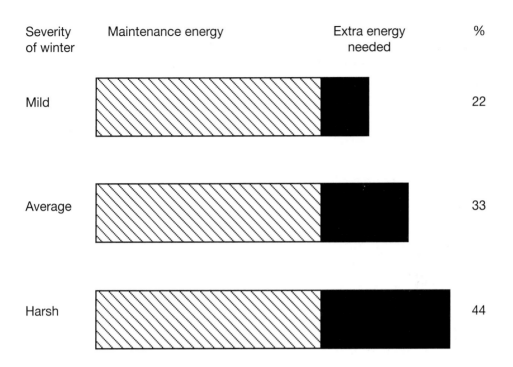

Severity of winter	Maintenance energy	Extra energy needed	%
Mild			22
Average			33
Harsh			44

Fig 26 Effect of severity of winter on extra feed energy required by an outwintered, unprotected 400kg horse.

to 30 per cent can lead to heating, with temperatures rising to between 35 and 40°C. Hazardous contamination can occur at these temperatures.

- Baling at 35 to 50 per cent moisture can lead to spontaneous heating, 50 to 60°C being commonly achieved. Massive contamination can occur at these temperatures.

Dust mites are also a problem because they are potentially allergenic to both humans and horses. They are dependent on fungal spores for food, and in time may effect a decrease in spore numbers. However, the spores will be replaced by clumps of semi-digested spores in the form of mite excre-ment. It may be possible to distinguish mites in stored hay, or they may have disappeared leaving their excrement behind which is conclusive evidence of their former pres-ence. Hay which contains large numbers of mites or their excrement, even in the absence of large numbers of spores, is of poor quality and should not be fed to horses.

The Effects of Mould

Chronic obstructive pulmonary disease (COPD), commonly referred to as 'broken wind', often results from exposure to mouldy hay that contains a large number of fungal spores. When a horse pulls on dry

A New Zealand rug is essential to the comfort of the horse outwintered at grass, and its use will significantly reduce feeding costs.

hay these fungal spores are exploded into the atmosphere, which means that he cannot avoid inhaling them. Some horses are so hypersensitive to these spores that they experience asthma-type symptoms after inhaling them. Over time, this disease leads to a loss of condition and performance.

The consequences of supplying mouldy feed to your horse are all too clear and should therefore be avoided at all costs. First, it may result in a coughing and ailing horse due to respiratory problems; and second, as the nutritional status of the feed is likely to be less, your horse will lose condition: all of which will cost you far in excess of the price of good quality feed in the first place. Clean, quality feed is an investment and you should spend some time in ensuring you are getting what you pay for.

Nutritive Value

Hay can be used to supply a proportion, or all (usually between 30 to 100 per cent) of the horse's diet, depending on his workload. However, this does not represent the proportion of nutrient requirements that are being met. For example, the hay may supply the total energy requirements of the horse, but meet only 80 per cent of his protein requirements, leaving a deficit of 20 per cent protein. Similarly, it is highly unlikely that micronutrient requirements will also be met in full; the proportion of requirements that are met will depend on whether the hay is of good or poor quality.

Simply because you provide a plentiful supply of hay for your horse, it does not necessarily follow that his nutrient requirements will be fulfilled. There can be drastic nutrient shortages on 'all-hay' diets, as well as nutrient imbalances; a disturbance in the normal calcium-to-phosphorus ratios, for example.

By contrast, the diet of a performance horse is designed so that large quantities of concentrates are fed, with only the minimum of hay. In such cases, where hay accounts for only a small proportion of the food given, it will have less influence on nutrient intake than an all-hay diet; but it is nevertheless still important.

It is therefore crucial to realize then, that it is not the quantity of hay that is fed which is important in meeting the nutrient requirements of the horse, but the nutritional value, irrespective of whether the horse is being maintained on hay alone or on a mixed hay/concentrate diet.

HAY ALTERNATIVES

Hay can be considered to provide two things: indigestible fibre, or 'bulk' as it is known, and digestible nutrients. In the absence of quality hay it is a rational approach to seek alternative sources of fibre to ensure adequate gut function, and other sources of nutrients to meet bodily requirements.

Probably the cheapest source of long fibre in the UK is straw. While feeding straw to horses is quite alien to many owners, the use of good quality oat or barley straw, which will provide the necessary fibre, is worthy of consideration. Wheat straw is not a suitable alternative as it is generally too fibrous for feeding, although it is used in some chops.

It is not widely known that the energy content of mature timothy hay is often only equivalent to that of good quality spring barley straw, which may contain quite a lot of grass anyway if undersown. Many owners now include molassed chaff in their horse's feed as 'bulk', without stopping to think that what they are actually feeding is chopped, molassed straw, which may or may not have had the addition of some minerals. These chaff products often contain up to 40 per cent molasses and in spite of this high level, remain remarkably 'unsticky'. While horses seem to like these products, they are deficient in protein and contain high levels of potassium which has a diuretic effect (causing excessive urination).

Straw-Based Diets

To determine the value of straw it is necessary to consider its nutrient content and compare it with hay (*see* Table 10.3).

In the past, owners often fed large quantities of oat straw to farm horses without any undue effects. Nowadays oat straw is not so freely available, and in any case there seems to be a reluctance to use straw other than in the guise of molassed chaff. However, if any difficulty is experienced in obtaining good quality hay then the use of straw as an alternative is worthy of consideration. Straw has the advantage over hay in that it is harvested at a drier time of year; consequently it is usually fairly easy to obtain 'clean' supplies of barley and oat straw. Obviously such straws are generally lower in protein, energy and some minerals, such as phosphorus, than hay, but as long as these deficiencies are recognized it is easy to balance the ration as necessary (*see* Chapter 14).

Bagged Grass Products

The remaining source of fibre, apart from farm silages, is that provided by semi-wilted, bagged grass products. These are expensive, and another disadvantage is the variable quality between bags and the consequential effects on nutrient intake. This variability in intake is undesirable and is difficult to control with these types of products.

How Much to Feed

Having selected the most appropriate foodstuffs, the next step it to decide how much the horse needs to be fed. The simplest approach is initially to base the feeding programme on the bodyweight of the horse. Generally, energy needs are related to bodyweight when considering a maintenance diet. The weight of a horse can be obtained using a specialized horse weigher or a lorry weighbridge; however, it is not always easy to gain access to such facilities, so the simplest and quickest method is to take the measurement of the *heart girth*. This can be done using a specially produced weigh-tape for horses or an ordinary measuring tape. Take a measurement all the way round your horse just behind his withers, then use the data in Table 10.4 to give a fairly good estimation of your horse's weight.

Armed with a figure for your horse's total bodyweight, you can then begin to work out his total daily feed requirements. Usually this is between 1.75 and 2.5 per cent of his bodyweight for dry feeds (*see* Table 10.6), although the

Table 10.3 Nutrient characteristics of straws and hay expressed on the basis of per kg as fed

	Digestible energy (MJ/kg)	Protein (g/kg)	Fibre (g/kg)
Grass hay	7–8	40–80	320–350
Barley straw	6	35	410
Oat straw	6	45	400
Wheat straw	5	30	420

How to Feed Straw

The practical aspect of offering straw to a horse might seem obvious, but most owners shy away from simply giving it as it comes from the bale. However, the inclusion of straw in the ration becomes very expensive if it has to be processed into a chaff and this is, in any case, unnecessary. Why go to all that trouble when the horse is equipped with his very own effective grinding mechanism (molar and premolar teeth, see Chapter 3). There are other benefits, too, in employing the horse to process long straw for himself: by doing so he will be occupied for a large part of his time and this will reflect his natural eating pattern, which may go some way to preventing vices such as weaving and crib-biting. Also, because straw is eaten slowly but with an increased chewing activity, he will produce large volumes of saliva which contribute significantly to his overall well-being.

Straw mixes

Straw may also be used in combination with artificially dehydrated alfalfa or grass and molasses, utilizing the concept that an equal mix of dried grass (which contains 16 per cent protein) and straw is equivalent in terms of nutrients to a hay of reasonable quality. Both chopped, dried alfalfa and chopped dried grass would provide sufficient fibre for maintenance feeding, although there would be an excess of protein. Dried alfalfa and grass are readily available in pelleted form and may be fed as a 'complete' diet, although it would be better if the raw material was not ground before pelleting.

You may feel that if high quality hay cannot be obtained, providing the horse with his total feed allowance in pellet form is the ideal alternative. Unfortunately however, there are drawbacks. First, a greedy horse may bolt his food as quickly as possible, with the risk that he might choke. This problem can be avoided to some extent by using only 3mm pellets. Where a horse is known to bolt his feed, the problem can be totally overcome by soaking the pellets for a few hours in water before feeding. Second, this type of forage supply should not be offered ad-lib to a stabled horse because it would supply an excess of nutrients. Thus the horse will eat his allowance quickly when it is offered, with the unfortunate consequence that he will be standing idle for much of the day, a circumstance that can lead to abnormal behaviour or stable vices, such as wood-chewing.

actual amount of feed needed by your horse will depend on his individual type and will also be affected by his temperament. No two horses are the same, so one 500kg (10cwt) horse will often need a different quantity of food to another 500kg horse to remain in similar condition. How often have you heard the expression 'I can't keep the weight on my horse'? This type of animal is often more active and perhaps more 'highly strung' than his stable companion who may be a 'good doer'. There is no such thing as 'feeding by the book', so recognizing

Table 10.4 Correlation between heart-girth measurement (cm) and weight (kg)

Girth measurement (cm)	Approximate liveweight (kg)
128	182
140	227
148	273
156	318
164	364
171	409
178	455
185	500
192	545
197	591

WHEN TO FEED CONCENTRATES

As soon as horses undertake some work, owners automatically assume that they will have to add concentrates to their horse's ration. This is simply not the case, however, and many horses can perform quite a lot of work without needing supplementary feeding. Remember that 'excess' of nutritional requirements we discussed at the beginning of the chapter? This will need to be used up first before a situation arises where the horse needs something 'extra'. Obviously it is essential to monitor your horse's weight continuously, because no matter how well trained the eye is, bodyweight change is never noticed until it has happened, which is too late!

The nutritional quality of the hay provided will feature strongly in the decision as to whether or not to add concentrates to the feed. Take as an example a 500kg (10cwt) horse consuming 2.5 per cent of his bodyweight in hay. If this hay was of average quality he would be ingesting about 135 per cent of his *predicted* maintenance energy requirements. This amount would be considered to be sufficient to support light work as well as maintenance, which in reality is all most 'weekend' horses do. In contrast, hay of poor quality fed at that level might be insufficient for even maintenance purposes and some concentrate might be necessary. The key to recognizing the need for concentrate is first, an appreciation of hay quality and second, monitoring of the horse's weight. The latter may

when feed quantity needs altering is very important. Let your horse be your guide. Keep a constant check on his condition, as it may change gradually without you being aware: is he dropping off a bit? Does he look a bit podgy? When you are around your horse every day you may fail to recognize any change in his weight, so make a point of taking a second look every week, and remeasure him from time to time as a routine procedure.

Taking average daily feeding requirements based on the 1.75 to 2.5 per cent of liveweight as your guide, you will be able to budget roughly for the quantity of forage your horse will require. If storage is not a problem, then bulk buying is possible and better prices can often be negotiated, as well as better quality consignments of hay.

be easy to do, but the former is perhaps more difficult.

In order to assess hay quality the following points should be considered:

1. **Stage of growth**: a great many mature seeded heads indicate the grass was cut at a very late stage of growth and is thus of low value.
2. **Quantity of leaf**: a lot of leaf is desirable since it is nutrient rich and easily digested.
3. **Colour**: green is preferred as it indicates rapid making and therefore minimal field losses.
4. **Identity of plant species**: Italian and perennial ryegrasses are preferred to fescues, cock's-foot and timothy.

HOW MUCH CONCENTRATE?

As indicated, this will depend on forage quality, and also on the intensity and duration of the work the horse performs. Feeding rates must be adjusted to maintain the horse's condition and weight, and this may be achieved by increasing or reducing the total ration (forage *and* concentrates) within the constraints of the horse's appetite. Alternatively, the forage-to-concentrate ratios may be altered (usually by

Table 10.5 Typical forage:concentrate ratios

	Forage	Concentrates
Rest/light work	1–0.7	0–0.3
Moderate work	0.7–0.5	0.3–0.5
Hard work	0.3–0.5	0.7–0.5

raising the concentrate level and lowering the forage level). Typical ratios are shown in Table 10.5.

How much concentrate is needed is based on the need to fulfil the energy and protein requirements of the horse, which increase in relation to his stage of development or his workload.

When considering forage quality, the amount of protein present in hay needs to be evaluated. The protein content of hays is very variable, although most grass hays will contain between 4 and 8 per cent. Thus, hay of poor quality will require some supplementation, even for a horse at maintenance. This may be achieved in a variety of ways:

1. By supplementing with low protein compound, for example, by using a mixture of 64 per cent hay (containing 4 per cent protein) and 36 per cent com-

Table 10.6 Maintenance diet, showing proportions of hay and concentrate, and protein supplied

Intake (% of liveweight)	Diet proportions (%)		Protein (%)
	Concentrate	Hay	
1.75–2.5	0	100	7–8

pound (containing 12 per cent protein). This amounts to feeding in the proportion of 640g (1.7lb) of hay and 360g (13oz) of compound to each kilogram of the horse's total ration.

2. By supplementing with straight cereal: for example, a mixture of 46 per cent hay and 54 per cent oats would meet the protein requirements of the horse, but this would also result in excessive amounts of energy being supplied, which is undesirable to a horse at maintenance.

3. By supplementing with a concentrate such as soya, which would minimize excess energy intake. The correct mixture would be 93 per cent hay (containing 4 per cent protein) and 7 per cent soya (containing 44 per cent protein). This amounts to 930g (2lb) of hay and 70g (2.5oz) of soya per kilogram of feed.

4. By using a protein-rich forage. If 16 per cent dried grass is available, then a mixture containing 76 per cent hay and 24 per cent dried grass would be ideal to achieve an overall dietary protein level of 6.88 per cent. This option is probably the best where hay is of poor quality, especially for horses kept at maintenance where it is important to use high fibre/low energy feeds.

It is not true to say that hay always needs supplementation, however. In many instances, protein requirements can be met in full by certain types of hay alone. Legume hay usually contains much more protein than do grass hays, and grass/clover mixtures are somewhere between the two, containing anywhere between 6 and 10 per cent protein.

Summary Points

- Hay quality is variable depending on when and how it was made.
- It is important to select hay of high nutritional value and hygienic quality.
- The use of unprocessed straw allows horse owners to provide fibre for their animals more cheaply than relying on the conventional forage hay when it is in short supply.
- This somewhat unconventional approach will be successful provided rations are formulated in the knowledge that straw is not a good source of all nutrients.
- The requirements of outwintered horses will depend on the severity of the winter, although the quantity of food required can be significantly reduced by the provision of a rug and shelter.
- Feed requirement is related to bodyweight which should be carefully assessed and then monitored to confirm the adequacy of energy intake.
- The use of concentrates will be regulated by the quality of the forage source, and the stage of the horse's development or his workload.
- Alternative high quality forages can be used in the maintenance ration to avoid or limit the use of concentrates.
- The purchase of good quality forages can obviate the need to use concentrates and will therefore effect significant cost savings for horses doing little or no work.

11

FEEDING FOR
BREEDING & GROWTH

Feeds and feeding are important components of successful breeding programmes. Other vital factors including day length and temperature, which to a certain extent can be managed to improve conception rates, and there are some factors which can be influenced by the veterinarian involved. Nutrition can affect both the broodmare and the stallion, although often the latter receives only scant attention because of his fleeting involvement.

NUTRITION OF THE BROODMARE

During the first eight months of the mare's eleven-month pregnancy there is little foetal growth, and if she is not already supporting a foal then to all intents and purposes she may be fed as a gelding at maintenance. Some in-foal mares continue to be worked early in pregnancy, when the quality and quantity of food provided will be dictated by the work performed. The nature of the diet provided during the last ninety days of the pregnancy will greatly depend on the date of conception. An early conception in late winter will result in a mid-winter foal the following year, when only conserved food is available; late conception in early summer will mean a late spring foal which coincides with fresh grass prior to, and after foaling.

The growth of the foal will be affected by the quality and quantity of feed given to the mare, coupled with the efficiency with which nutrients are transferred from the maternal blood supply to that of the foal. A healthy, well-formed placenta is essential for this latter process to be effective. It has also been suggested that the age of the mare may play a part, with young and older mares producing lighter foals than those of middle age. Over the last ninety days of pregnancy the mare will require additional energy, although what is required is not that great and many owners

Table 11.1 Pregnancy diet, showing proportions of hay and concentrate, and protein supplied

Months	Intake (% of liveweight)	Diet proportions (%)		Protein (%)
		Concentrate	Hay	
9	1.5–2	20	80	9
10	1.5–2	20	80	9.5
11	1.5–2	30	70	10

overfeed at this time. The mare does not need to be provided with a great deal more than her normal maintenance needs, only remembering that as her weight increases so will her maintenance needs.

This apparently simple picture of pregnancy feeding is complicated by the fact that the developing foal will occupy an increasing proportion of the mare's abdominal cavity, thereby reducing her capacity for bulky feedstuffs. As capacity declines, nutrient requirements increase, and thus you will have to feed 'quality' rather than 'quantity'.

Early feeding management of the mare should revolve around the provision of a balanced diet and supplying sufficient energy to maintain an appropriate body condition. Many owners and managers are aware that mares in poor condition or those that are losing condition are not very successful breeders, whereas overweight mares or those in very good condition do not appear to be disadvantaged in the same way. The best advice is therefore to try to maintain mares in a 'fit' condition: neither too fat, nor too thin. If outwintered, particular care will have to be taken to ensure that the mare consumes adequate energy. This will be required to sustain the continued growth of the foal, and to maintain the mare; the latter will depend first on her size, and second on the ambient temperature. Low temperatures in combination with rain and wind can double the mare's energy requirements. It will be most beneficial if the mare has access to a good field shelter and is also rugged, such strategies serving to increase her comfort and reduce the feed bill! Although large mares will require more energy to maintain themselves, they are generally less badly affected by inclement weather conditions. The energy requirements of a small mare will increase proportionately much more quickly than those of a large mare when both are exposed to worsening weather conditions. With a mixed group of mares this can present problems, since the bigger mares may bully the smaller ones away from supplementary feeding, and yet it is their need which is the greatest. Smaller mares will therefore benefit from being fed separately.

High fibre, low energy roughages such as straw chops are inappropriate for feeding during the last three months of pregnancy. Good quality roughage containing digestible fibre is essential, and in most cases it will be necessary to feed concentrates as well. Horses should drink 2 to 5 litres (3½ to 8 pints) per kilogram of dry food, and while everyone appreciates that horses, like ourselves, drink more when it is hot, few appreciate that voluntary drinking can be markedly reduced by low temperatures. Under-drinking can lead to implication colics in pregnant mares because the gut contents 'dry out', and this is much more likely if high fibre roughage is fed. To some extent this problem can be alleviated if succulent feeds are incorporated in the ration; a good example would be silage which may contain from 50 to 75 per cent water. Hay and concentrate feeds usually only contain about 12 per cent water, which is radically different from the material that the horse has evolved to eat – grass. Thus, the nature of the diet can have a substantial effect on the water balance of the mare and her need to drink.

Typical rations for a 550kg (10cwt) broodmare during the months of pregnancy are shown in Table 11.2. It will be apparent that the quality of the roughage has a great effect on the composition of the ration, and poor quality hay necessitates the use of more concentrate. Ration 1 would require supplementation with micronutrients in spite of the fact that the major nutrients are supplied. Combinations of feeds can be used, although simplicity is probably better in that it is easier to achieve a balanced diet. Thus a good quality cube will supply all the vitamins and minerals required by the mare, so that feeding supplements is not necessary.

A 500kg (10cwt) mare will produce about 20kg (44lb) of milk per day, and although it is of relatively poor quality, it effectively doubles the need for food energy as compared to maintenance levels. Late foaling mares will obtain all their energy, protein, calcium and phosphorus needs from good quality pasture, in spite of the fact that their protein needs will have increased. If, however, grass supplies are limited or of dubious quality, then supplementary feeding will be required to avoid the mare losing too much weight and jeopardizing milk supplies.

The choice of supplementary feed is regulated by the availability of grass. Moderate supplies of grass can be augmented with some cereal or perhaps a

---

Table 11.2 Specimen rations for a 550kg broodmare in the last month of pregnancy

(Appetite assumed to be about 9kg per day.)

Ration 1	Ration 2	Ration 3
2kg oats	3kg stud cubes	5kg stud cubes
7kg alfalfa	6kg good hay	4kg poor hay

---

combination of cereal and some basic horse and pony nuts. Poor quality grass resources would necessitate using stud nuts that contain quite a lot of protein (16–18 per cent).

NUTRITION OF THE STALLION

Diets for stallions should be based on roughage and if this is good quality, it can form the greater part of the ration. The best guide is to consider that the horse is doing light work and feed accordingly. However, individuality plays an important part in stallion maintenance. Some stallions fret and become very restless during the covering season and can expend quite a lot of energy just pacing up and down. In such circumstances it may be necessary to feed some compound which will ensure adequate micronutrient intakes. Obviously the extra energy supplied will be beneficial to such horses, and in fact it may be necessary to feed quite a lot of 'extra' concentrate. Thus the character of the stallion must be assessed when designing appropriate rations to try to ensure that he is neither under- nor overfed energy, and that he receives a balanced diet containing an adequate supply of micronutrients, whatever the composition of the daily ration.

The frequency with which the mare suckles her foal progressively decreases as the foal ages.

Table 11.3 Lactation diet, showing proportions of hay and concentrate, and protein supplied

Stage	Intake (% of liveweight)	Diet proportions (%) Concentrate	Hay	Protein (%)
Foaling to 12 weeks	2 – 3	50	50	12
12 weeks to weaning	2 – 2.5	35	65	10

NUTRITION AND DEVELOPMENT OF FOALS AND YOUNGSTOCK

Initial feeding of the foal is the responsibility of the mare whose feeding management has been described. While in the womb, the foetus enjoys a continuous supply of nutrients via the placenta. Following birth, the body of the newborn foal must adapt quickly from relying on intravenous feeding, to coping with an intermittent supply of nutrients in the form of ingested milk via the gut, and its growth, development and health depend upon how well its gut responds to this new source.

Milk composition reflects the stage of development and the nutritional needs of the foal at birth. The first milk, or colostrum, contains a lot of protein and the foal depends on this to confer immunity against a number of disease organisms; he needs to receive colostrum within thirty-six hours of birth, otherwise he will be susceptible to gastro-enteritis and septicaemia. Thus the neonatal foal is at considerable risk if not suckled by the mare during the immediate postnatal period. After this period the protein content of the milk declines. Soon after birth foals begin to graze, although they will continue to suck for several months. 'Normal' mare's milk is high in carbohydrate and low in protein and fat: after the postnatal period the decline in protein is accompanied by a rise in the quantity of milk produced by the mare, and this ensures that the foal receives a high energy intake during the first months of lactation. (Additional water of about 50 litres/11 gallons per day is required by the mare in order to support an average milk yield.)

Lactation and Foal Growth

Sucking frequency is very high initially, but becomes less as the foal ages. Young foals suck for quite a short period on each occasion, and thus ingest relatively small quantities of milk at a time. If the mare produces significantly less milk than the foal needs, then obviously growth rates will be affected. In this eventuality, the provision of creep feed based on dried skimmed milk is a good idea. This can be introduced from twenty-four days of age, and hopefully as a result, normal growth rates will then be achieved and maintained. A mare's milk will be adequate for the first twelve weeks of a foal's life, although during this period the foal will begin to eat pasture grass, hay and any concentrates being given to the mare.

An average growth rate for Thoroughbred foals while nursing would be 1–1.5kg (2–3lb) per day, although this will be affected by the quantity of milk produced by that mare and the availability of creep feed. Unfortunately, skeletal defects in foals are quite common, and include physitis, angular deformities, osteochondrosis dissecans, malformation of the cervical vertebra ('wobblers'), and carpus. A number of different factors have been implicated, including nutrition, heredity, exercise and conformation. Inbreeding within the Thoroughbred industry may improve the chances of producing horses of high athletic ability, but it means that less desirable traits may be concentrated in the offspring.

CREEP FEEDING

The effect of creep feeding on the skeletal growth and bone development of nursing Thoroughbred, Quarter Horse, or cross foals has been examined. Over a four-month period, creep-fed foals (fed creep at 1.5 per cent of liveweight), gained 133kg (293lb), whereas those not receiving creep gained only 117kg (257lb). The difference in liveweight gain between the two groups on a daily basis was not large: the creep-fed animals gained 1.1kg (2lb 4oz) per day, compared to 0.98kg (2lb) per day for the unsupplemented group. Maximum rates of gain were achieved during the first five weeks of life when those receiving creep feed gained an average of 1.31kg (2lb 13oz) compared to 1.08kg (2lb 6oz) per day for the other group. In spite of the fact that the mares would be producing large amounts of milk during the first 100 days of lactation, supplemental nutrition produced a significant growth response in the foals. Wither height increased more rapidly in the first 100 days of life in foals fed creep; however, after 130 days there was no difference in wither height between the groups of foals.

The effect of creep-feeding suckling foals is to increase rate of growth, and examination of bone indicated little decrease in quality. The extra nutrients supplied by the creep appeared to maintain skeletal growth in faster-growing animals. However, the proportion of cortical bone in the new bone that was formed was slightly less in creep-fed foals than in slower-growing foals. Thus it would appear that foals fed for rapid growth may not maximize bone deposition and that care needs to be taken to provide creep that contains the appropriate nutrients; oats alone would be inappropriate because they do not contain a balanced supply of minerals.

Weaning

Natural weaning normally takes place when the foal is a year or more old, or when the mare foals again. Thoroughbred foals are weaned at a much younger age, often between four and six months. Weaning at this young age is clearly stressful, as evidenced by the noise the foals make on enforced separation and their attempts to get back to their mothers. Such is their desperation to do this that they sometimes injure themselves in the process. A temporary loss of appetite and a subsequent reduction in growth rate is frequently observed in newly weaned foals.

There have been a few attempts to determine methods of weaning that minimize the stress on the foal. A comparison between weaning foals individually into boxes or in pairs indicated that weaning in pairs was less stressful. Other methods contrast abrupt, complete separation of the mare and foal to gradual separation methods in which the mare and foal retain sight, sound and smell contact, but in which suckling is prevented. It is consistently found that the first method is more stressful, and that creep-feeding prior to weaning does not appear to alleviate the problem.

An interesting discovery resulting from one study was that foals not fed any creep prior to weaning had a much higher intake of creep post-weaning than those that were, and as a consequence they grew more quickly. Foals that were weaned by gradual or partial separation ate more than those animals that were abruptly weaned, and maintained a consistent growth rate. Foals that were abruptly weaned showed hormonal changes indicative of stress and which, in other species, has been associated with lowered resistance to disease.

Table 11.4 Proportion (%) of mature weight achieved at 6, 12 and 18 months of age by different horse types

Type	Months		
	6	12	18
Thoroughbreds	46	67	80
Quarter Horses	44	63	79
Arabs	46	66	80
Half-Arabs/Anglo-Arabs	45	67	81
Ponies (mature weight 180kg)	55	75	84
Percherons	38	55	73
Draught Horses	34	52	69

Table 11.5 Proportion (%) of mature height achieved at 6, 12 and 18 months of age by different horse types

Type	Months		
	6	12	18
Thoroughbreds	83	90	95
Quarter Horses	84	91	95
Half-Arabs/Anglo-Arabs	83	92	95

Growth Rate

It is currently thought that controlling liveweight gain in foals will go some way to reducing the problem of metabolic bone disease. More and more studs now weigh their foals as an aid to management and try to obtain consistent gain rather than allow growth spurts. Available data, by which to make judgements on what is an appropriate rate of growth, is limited. If the average mature weight of a Thoroughbred stallion is taken to be 550kg (11cwt), and that of a mare 500kg (10cwt), then it might be expected that foals would achieve liveweights equivalent to 46, 67 and 80 per cent of mature weight at six, eight and twelve months respectively. Table 11.4 provides an interesting comparison between different horse types in this respect.

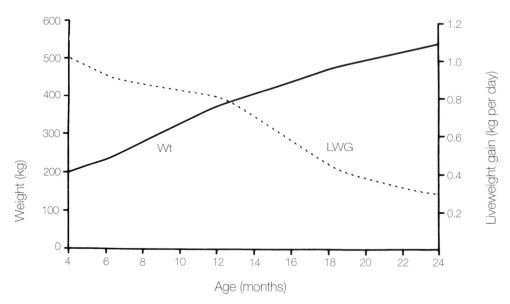

Fig 27 Foal growth.

There is a remarkable consistency between the light horse breeds, and these values might reasonably be used as guides for their rate of development. The large draught horses reach their mature weights later than light horses, although they still have the capacity for rapid liveweight gain when young and care is needed to avoid 'pushing' them too hard.

Table 11.5 provides a comparison between breeds in terms of the height they achieve at the same time intervals used in Table 11.4. It is clear from this information that the values are remarkably uniform and can provide another 'yardstick' for appropriate rates of development. The mature height for Thoroughbreds can be assumed to be about 162cm (16hh.) for stallions and 160cm (15.3hh.) for mares. Consideration of

both tables shows that by eighteen months of age Thoroughbreds have nearly achieved their full height, but only four-fifths of their mature weight. What is crucial to these animals is that the bone is fully mineralized and able to carry the additional musculature that develops with training. The greatest amount of bone elongation occurs during the first few months of life, which emphasizes the need for a balanced supply of nutrients. In one study on a Thoroughbred stud in Canada, colts weighed 55kg (121lb) at birth and fillies 54kg (119lb). Colts were generally heavier, taller and bigger-boned than fillies, and the differences increased with time. Mares less than seven years of age had smaller foals, and this might reflect the decreased ability of the younger mare to provide nutrients to

Table 11.6 Growth diet, showing proportions of hay and concentrate, and protein supplied

Age	Total intake (% of liveweight)	Diet proportions (%)		Protein (%)
		Concentrate	Hay	
0–3 months	2.5–3.5	100	0	16
Weaning	2.5–3.5	70	30	13
12 months	2–3	60	40	12
18 months	2–2.5	50	50	11
24 months	2–2.5	50	50	10

the developing foetus. It is clear that factors such as sex of the foal, age of the mare, and the month of birth, can influence characteristics in the foal, such as weight, height at withers, circumference of the cannon bone, and so on.

Cattle have been rigorously selected for growth rate so that they are ready for slaughter between ten and eighteen months of age at weights equivalent to those of Thoroughbred racehorses. Although racehorses often race as two-year-olds, they have not been deliberately bred for growth and yet they show rates of body gain similar to that in suckled calves of large-breed crosses. These developing calves do not demonstrate the metabolic bone disorders that develop in Thoroughbred foals. Stress on limb bones occurs when increase in bodyweight per unit increase in height is large, and yet calves escape the problems endured by foals. This may be because foals are fed home-made diets that fail to meet their nutrient needs. Furthermore these diets are usually based on poor quality roughage (hay) where both protein content and quality are low.

Attempts have been made to investigate the role of feed restriction on yearling development. Comparisons between yearlings fed *ad libitum* and those restricted to 80 per cent of the energy intake showed that animals fed *ad libitum* gained 85kg (187lb) in 140 days, while those in the other group gained 67kg (148lb) in the same period. The gain in wither height was virtually unaffected. Other studies have demonstrated that energy or protein deprivation affects bodyweight gain more severely than body height gain. Thus, length of bone does not appear to be greatly influenced by periods of deprivation, but quality of bone may be compromised; long-term deprivation can lead to stunting.

Practical Feeding of Youngstock

A rough guide to feeding foals is to feed 450g (1lb) of creep feed per day for every month of age. For example, a two-month-old foal will be fed 900g (2lb) of creep feed per day, a four-month-old foal 1,800g (4lb), and so on. The importance of encouraging foals to consume dry feed while nursing

Table 11.7 A growth comparison between suckled and artificially reared foals and the consumption of milk substitute and creep by the artificially reared foals (all values in kg)

	Suckled foals		Artificially reared foals		Daily food consumption of artificially reared foals	
Week	Liveweight	Daily gain	Liveweight	Daily gain	Milk substitute	Creep
1	59.2	1.7	56.3	0.7	12.6	–
2	71.0	1.2	61.6	0.9	15.1	0.06
3	79.7	1.5	67.6	1.1	16.6	0.17
4	90.2	1.7	75.5	1.3	19.4	0.21
5	97.1	1.0	84.6	1.3	21.7	0.30
6	103.9	1.4	92.6	1.1	22.0	0.40
7	113.8	1.4	100.4	1.2	24.9	0.56
8	122.9	1.5	108.9	1.6	27.2	0.71

cannot be over-emphasized. Foals that do not consume adequate amounts of feed while nursing are at a higher risk of developing orthopaedic disorders after weaning than those that do.

The best way to feed youngstock over their first winter is to provide a constant supply of chopped forage and concentrate because this avoids the post-feeding peaks of insulin associated with 'meal' feeding (*see* Chapter 4). Extruded concentrate may be helpful in that food intake is slowed and some of the starch is broken down, thereby facilitating digestion and reducing the risk of digestive disorders.

During their second season at grass the intake of grass by yearlings appears to be most affected by the quantity of material on offer. For example, it has been demonstrated that yearlings which have available to them about 500kg (10cwt) of grass per day gained 0.48kg (1lb 1oz) per day, whereas those with access to only half as much grass, gained only 0.25 kg (9oz) per day. To maximize growth rates at grass, excessive amounts of herbage must be offered, approximately fifteen times that which is required; and also, grass alone is inadequate to support *maximum* growth rates. **It should be emphasized, however, that maximum does not necessarily equate to desirable.** The likely forage contribution of the ration over the first twenty-four months is summarized in Table 11.6.

Artificial Rearing

Most powdered milk replacers contain about 13 per cent fat and 22 to 25 per cent protein on a dry basis, which closely resembles the composition of mare's milk on the same basis. Most manufacturers suggest that their products should be diluted 1 part powder to 4 parts water, which yields a concentration of about 25 per cent dry matter. While this is all right for the the first few days of life, it is quite different from normal mare's milk, which contains about 10 per cent dry matter. Furthermore, the fat and protein levels would approach 4 and 6 per cent respectively, which are much higher than the levels of 1.5 and 2 per cent found in normal milk. Milk powder should initially be diluted 1 in 4 and then gradually changed to 1 in 10 to produce a final composition that parallels mare's milk. There is some evidence to suggest that the concentration of dry matter in milk replacers can affect the frequency of scouring in calves and thus it might be unwise to supply concentrated milk substitutes to foals.

A recent study showed that foals artificially reared on milk substitute, diluted 1 in 10 and fed at no more than 25 per cent of liveweight per day, performed almost as well as their naturally suckled counterparts. The amounts fed were adjusted twice weekly according to changes in bodyweight. Creep was introduced during week 2 up to 1 per cent of bodyweight, and grass/legume hay was available from week 3.

It will be apparent from Table 11.7 that over the first two weeks the suckled foals grew much more quickly, and this leads to a discrepancy in liveweight which persists over the measurement period, although the average daily gain of the artificially reared groups soon achieved normal rates.

Foal diarrhoea was mild and in some animals did not begin until the second week of feeding; this corresponded with the scours that occurred in the normally suckled foals. It was concluded that the diarrhoea was not a consequence of the milk replacer but more probably of the initial migration of worm larvae (*Strongyloides westerii*). Furthermore, the provision of plenty of fluid minimized the risk of dehydration which would be more likely in foals fed concentrated milk replacers. Artificially reared foals should have access to fresh faeces from a healthy adult horse which has been wormed regularly. This will enable the establishment of desirable bacterial flora in the foal's intestinal tract. (Suckled foals will frequently be observed consuming fresh faecal material while at grass). In addition, good-quality probiotics can be used although it is important to ensure that effective strains of organisms are present and that they are present as *viable* cells, preferably in large numbers. Some studs administer probiotics routinely to newborn foals within the first eight hours of birth and then again a few days later. During the first few days of life, the gut flora of the foal is unstable and thus more susceptible to dietary and environmental influences. However, it should be remembered that the best and most effective method of administering probiotics is continuous daily feeding, which ensures that the organisms are present in the gut in large numbers and are able to metabolize and produce their probiotic effect.

After eight weeks of age, or even earlier, the quantity of milk replacer can be reduced gradually and the total feed allowance can be increased to about 2.5/3.5 per cent of bodyweight; the concentrate proportion will rarely exceed 2 per cent of bodyweight, and it is probably better to restrict it to 1 per cent or less, the remainder of the diet being made up of forage. Foals can safely be weaned once they are consuming at least 1 kg (2lb) of creep feed and about 0.5kg (1lb) of good-quality (preferably grass/legume) hay per day.

Summary Points

- Feeding the broodmare can be fairly simple provided good quality basal roughage is available. A 16–18 per cent protein concentrate may also be necessary; a purchased compound avoids the need for supplements.
- One concentrate can suffice for both pregnancy and lactation: although there is a large difference in nutrient needs, the proportion of concentrate fed in lactation is far greater than that used in pregnancy in normal circumstances.
- Thoroughbred mares will totally depend on us to provide the requisite nutrients due to their 'unnatural' breeding season.
- Non-Thoroughbred mares can usually depend on an almost natural supply of nutrients via grass, and can enjoy the freedom of grazing it.
- It is important to ensure that the overall quantity and quality of the diet is in keeping with the needs of the mare, at each stage of her reproductive cycle.
- The easiest approach to feeding the broodmare is to use a reputable stud cube in combination with good quality roughage. The quantities fed will have to be adjusted, first to be within the limits of appetite and second, not to create over-fatness.
- Young foals are dependent on their mothers for adequate nutrition.
- Underfeeding the mare can prejudice normal foal growth; yet it may be beneficial in preventing bone deformity in foals produced by very 'milky' mares.
- It is crucial that the foal suckles from the mare and obtains colostrum within the first thirty-six hours of life.
- Youngstock are fed a mixture of concentrate and roughage, and while it is important to encourage dry food intake, over-consumption of concentrate should be avoided.
- Food intake should be regulated to ensure a smooth growth curve.
- Creep-feeding preweaning is important to prevent overconsumption of creep after weaning, which can result in a growth spurt, and also to reduce the risk of orthopaedic disorders from developing.
- Feed restriction has its greatest effect on the attainment of body weight; growth in height is virtually unaffected.
- Parallel growth rates in other species where metabolic bone disease is not a problem suggests that more attention should be paid to the provision of balanced diets for mares and growing horses.
- Guidelines are available for monitoring the appropriate development of young stock and adherence to them may contribute to the reduction of orthopaedic problems.

12

FEEDING FOR
PERFORMANCE

While a horse cannot be fed to win, inadequate feeding can lead to substandard performance. Thus the objective when feeding the performance horse is to provide all the nutrients that his body requires for the biochemical processes which occur at cellular level. Work creates little extra demand for some nutrients, but a significantly increased need for others, arising either through greater internal use of nutrients or by their loss from the body in sweat.

NUTRIENT REQUIREMENTS

Protein: If energy intake is adequate, then in most cases exercising horses need relatively small amounts of protein over and above maintenance. However, this ignores the physiological and biochemical changes that occur in horses performing work. First, working horses consume more food than non-working horses; since internal losses of nitrogen increase with food intake, these have to be replaced. Second, some nitrogen is lost in sweat, and it is important to remember that a hard-worked horse can lose several kilograms of sweat during a period of exercise. Third, a greater amount of protein is taken up by the muscle tissue following exercise and during rest, so there is an increased need for protein.

There is a great debate over the relationship between protein intake and performance and no clear evidence has been produced to demonstrate that a high protein intake has a deleterious effect. However, there are guidelines based on the physiological and biochemical changes that occur during exercise. In working horses, and in particular endurance horses, the intake of more than 2g of digestible protein (about 3.5g dietary protein) per kilogram of bodyweight per day should be avoided for the following reasons:
1. Water requirements increase.
2. Urine flow rate decreases.

Table 12.1 Relationship between (i) weight and ration; (ii) ration composition and work

Weight (kg)	Daily ration (kg)	Medium work Roughage (kg)	Medium work Concentrate (kg)	Hard work Roughage (kg)	Hard work Concentrate (kg)
200	4	2	2	1.6	2.4
300	6	3	3	2.4	3.6
400	8	4	4	3.2	4.8
500	10	5	5	4.0	6.0
600	12	6	6	4.8	7.2

Table 12.2 Work diet, showing proportions of hay and concentrate, and protein supplied

Intensity	Intake (% of liveweight)	Diet proportions (%) Concentrate	Diet proportions (%) Hay	Protein (%)
Light	1.5–2.5	30	70	9
Moderate	1.75–2.75	50	50	9.5
Intense	2–3	70	30	10.55

3. Less urea is lost via the kidneys, and blood plasma urea levels increase.
4. More urea enters the gut and increases the risk of digestive disturbance.
5. More ammonia has to be detoxified in the liver which costs energy.
6. Ammonia levels increase in the peripheral blood, which can induce excitement and disrupt energy release.
7. High urinary nitrogen can lead to high atmospheric ammonia levels following urination, thereby stressing the respiratory system in stabled animals.

Calcium and Phosphorus: Losses via sweat are relatively small, so the require-ments of the exercising horse are only slightly higher than those for maintenance.

Trace minerals: The total dry matter intake of the exercising horse is higher than that of the non-working horse, so the amount of mineral eaten will be higher. Only small amounts of copper and zinc are lost in the sweat so no extra supply should be necessary. However, the need for iodine and selenium would be expected to increase with exercise, particularly as selenium is important for muscle function.

Vitamins A, D and K: Since these are not involved in energy turnover in muscle, higher intakes are necessary.

Energy: Physical demand can create a huge demand for energy, the type of activity affecting the magnitude of need. It is important to realize that energy expended during one day of hard exercise cannot be matched by the energy intake of that day. So the deficit must be made up by the mobilization of bodily energy stores. Energy stores are repleted on rest days; severe exercise may necessitate two to three days to recover pre-exercise levels of glycogen.

Sodium, Potassium and Chloride: Total requirements depend on the amount and the composition of the sweat produced.

Magnesium: This mineral is a component of several enzymes that are involved in energy release, and thus magnesium supplementation has been recommended to improve performance although only about 4g will be lost via sweat.

Iron: This is essential for the synthesis of haemoglobin and for replacing the small amount lost via sweat. Low haemoglobin values occur quite commonly in performance horses and are difficult to rectify.

Vitamin E: This is considered to be important in exercising horses. Undesirable biochemical changes occur when exercising, vitamin E-deficient horses.

Water-soluble vitamins: The daily administration of B-complex vitamins is a sensible strategy towards optimizing performance, as stress increases the horse's demand for these vitamins.

Electrolytes: These are crucial to the proper functioning of the body and in some respects we have yet to determine their role fully. Since they are of particular importance to the performance horse they will be discussed in detail here.

ELECTROLYTES

There is much confusion surrounding this topic. Although the term is frequently used, most horse owners have a poor understanding of what electrolytes are; and while owners appreciate that exercising horses that sweat creates special needs for electrolytes, they do not always realize that the horse requires electrolytes to be supplied on a daily basis.

Electrolytes are substances that dissolve in water and break down into their component parts. These parts – ions – are electrically charged and are either positive or negative, so an electrolyte solution can conduct electricity. There are many substances that dissolve in water and dissociate into electrically charged particles, but only a few are of significance to the horse.

Electrolytes with a positive charge are termed 'cations'; those with a negative charge 'anions'. It follows that the cations and anions must be in balance if neutrality is to be ensured: an excess of either one would create an acidic or basic environment. The most important cations are sodium, potassium, calcium, magnesium and phosphoric acid; the major anions are chloride and bicarbonate. The importance of these ions to the metabolism of the horse is acknowledged – for example, it is known that calcium has a crucial role in the formation and health of the skeletal system. Other roles, however, are less well known.

Balance of Cations and Anions

It is the relative quantities of cations and anions within a diet that determines the effect of that diet on an animal's chemistry. For example, the meat-rich diets of carnivores contain a lot of anions, so they are acidic; and this is apparent in the carnivore's acid urine. In contrast, the grass or hay diets of grazing herbivores – such as horses and cattle – contain more cations than anions, and so their diet is basic (alkaline) and they produce alkaline urine.

However, we manipulate the horse's diet to sustain the level of activity that we demand from him. As workload increases so does the quantity of concentrate that we feed, and this affects the balance of anions and cations in the diet. The addition of concentrates usually leads to a reduction of forage, and so the diet becomes increasingly acidic. The animal therefore has to buffer the dietary ionic imbalances.

The horse is well adapted to dealing with alkaline diets, so an acidic diet can create problems for a horse in that this acidity must be neutralized in the body. To do this effectively can mean that the animal has to mobilize his electrolyte reserves, and this can lead to demineralization of the bone: a serious consequence for a horse in whom skeletal strength is important.

As yet we do not fully understand the interactions between the electrolyte content of the diet and the metabolic reactions that occur in the body. Matters are further complicated when horses performing extended work sweat, losing electrolytes and altering the ion balance further still.

Sweating

During work, the body produces heat. As work rate increases, heat production increases correspondingly, causing the body's temperature to rise. At high temperatures, body processes will malfunction and the animal will die, so it is important that the body's temperature is prevented from rising by more than a few degrees. This is achieved through loss of moisture via the lungs, and by evaporation of sweat from the body's surface, during which process electrolytes are lost from the body.

Evaporation of sweat can be impaired in humid conditions where the evaporation rate – and thus cooling – is less effective. An hour of intermediate work will generate 'waste' heat equivalent to the energy contained in 5kg (11lb) of hay: this would require the evaporative loss of some 15 litres (26 pints) of water. But this assessment ignores factors such as ambient temperature, relative humidity, speed of movement, fitness, and so on. Horses that are used for sprinting lose relatively small volumes of water (about 5 litres/9 pints), although, once again, this can be affected by other factors.

Many people will have observed how some horses sweat up in the collecting ring prior to racing, and that others may sweat during transit. So it is conceivable that some horses may lose more water when they are excited. Deliberate withholding of water prior to racing or the failure of the horse to drink voluntarily during transit or at the stables – possible through stress – can complicate the electrolyte status of the horse.

Horses performing extended work can lose considerable volumes of water, particularly if ambient temperatures are high; unfit horses will sweat more and therefore lose more electrolytes than their fitter counterparts. Combined water losses can amount to 10–12 litres (18–21 pints) per hour, and total losses can exceed 40 litres (70 pints) per day. In an endurance horse weighing 500kg (10cwt), water losses can amount to 8–14 per cent of the total body water. These considerable losses will be reflected in a reduction in bodyweight and plasma volume; and bodyweight loss can be as high as 9 per cent, which in a 500kg horse amounts to 45kg (99lb).

Total body water is composed of intra-cellular fluid, extracellular fluid, and that which is present in the gut. The former two components are fairly constant, but the latter component can be manipulated by diet.

Water and Electrolyte Balance

The fluid held in the gut can act as a reserve for both water and electrolytes, and thus can offset the dehydrating effects of exercise. This compensatory effect can be exploited for the benefit of endurance horses where performance is limited not just by a shortage of energy but by a lack of water and electrolytes. The storage of water and electrolytes before an event can be influenced by the amount, type and composition of the feedstuffs offered (see Table 12.3).

Feeding should take place about four hours before the event so that energy is released from the food ingested at the time of feeding. Assuming *ad libitum* water intake is possible, horses will consume about 2.5kg of water per kilogram (2.5lb per pound) of dry matter ingested (equivalent to about 2.2kg of water per kilogram (0.54oz per pound) of hay or oats). About 80 per cent of water will be taken within four hours of consuming a meal.

Table 12.3 shows that potassium is lost quite quickly, while sodium is retained in the body much longer. Furthermore, horses fed Feed Type 1 will retain much more water and electrolytes than those fed Feed Type 2. It is probable that this store of water and electrolytes will be useful to the animal performing endurance work by improving the electrolyte balance. From the foregoing, it is possible to formulate a set of proposals for providing the best internal environment for work:

1. Feed 4–5 hours before the event.
2. Feed about 500g (1.1lb) of hay per 100kg (220lb) of liveweight. High potassium roughages such as alfalfa are not recommended because potassium intakes in excess of 150mg per kilogram of liveweight can stimulate a diuresis; grass hays should contain less than 20g per kilogram. Sugar-beet pulp (about 8g potassium per kg) may be mixed with the hay since it contains pectins (readily fermentation fibre), which release energy for several hours after consumption.
3. Feed 400g (13oz) concentrate per 100kg (220lb) of liveweight, and ensure that the sodium content exceeds 10g (0.35oz) per kilogram (1 per cent).

From these guidelines it will be apparent that a 500kg (10cwt) horse may be fed a meal of 2kg (2.2lb) concentrate and 2.5kg (5.5lb) roughage, ideally mixed together to ensure a plentiful salivary flow. Of course, free access to water should be guaranteed. The protein content of the concentrate should be minimized so that the overall protein of the roughage/concentrate mixture does not exceed 9 per cent: this will limit protein breakdown and so reduce the demands on the liver for removing ammonia.

Electrolytes in the Sweat

Average values can be used, although it must be appreciated that there is a large degree of variation in the quantities of sodium, potassium and chloride measured in sweat. For example, sodium concentrations have been shown to vary between 3 and 48 grams per litre (0.1 and 3oz per pint) although these are fairly extreme values. Reasonable mean values for sodium,

potassium and chloride would be 4, 2 and 8 grams per litre (0.2, 0.1 and 0.5oz per pint), respectively. A 500kg (10cwt) horse doing moderate work will lose, say, 5 litres (2 gallons) of sweat and this will contain 20, 10 and 40 grams per litre (0.7, 0.35 and 1.4oz) of sodium, potassium and chloride. Consideration of the sodium loss alone would require the feeding of 50g (1.8oz) of salt, which would incidentally supply 30g (1oz) of chloride; 10kg (22lb) of grass hay would supply between 10 and 20g (0.35 and 0.7oz) of sodium, and since, in our example, the horse is working then he might well be fed a 50:50 mix of hay and oats. This combina-

Table 12.3 Effect of type and composition of a feed on water and electrolyte balance in a 500kg horse

	Feed 1 2kg concentrates (5g sodium and 10g potassium/kg) 3kg hay (0.5g sodium and 20g potassium/kg)	Feed 2 2kg oats (0.5g sodium and 5g potassium/kg)
Intake		
Water (kg)	11.0	4.5
Sodium (g)	11.5	1.0
Potassium (g)	80.0	10.0
Loss after 4 hours		
Water (kg)	5.2	3.9
Sodium (g)	2.2	0.8
Potassium (g)	32.0	9.0
Retained		
Water (kg)	5.8	0.6
Sodium (g)	9.3	0.2
Potassium (g)	48.0	1.0

tion would supply between 6 and 13g (0.21 and 0.45oz) of sodium, and it is thus apparent that working horses fed oats and little or no compound will be very deficient in sodium. A working horse requires a minimum of 3g of sodium for every kilogram of feed, and this will not be adequate to balance any additional sodium lost via the sweat.

The horse has fairly substantial reserves of sodium, potassium and chloride that are readily exchangeable, i.e. available to replace losses through sweat, and these amount to approximately 340g, 1,000g and 400g (11, 34 and 13oz) respectively. Losses associated with 40 litres (9 gallons) of sweat during an endurance event, where the ambient temperature is high, could amount to 160g, 80g and 320g (5.6, 3 and 11oz) respectively. These quantities represent 0.47, 0.08 and 0.8 per cent of the exchangeable reserves, and it is clear that losses through sweat have their greatest effect on sodium and chloride metabolism.

The precise metabolic inter-relationships are complex, and there can be renal responses to electrolyte status. However, suffice to say that horses that sweat can lose substantial amounts of electrolytes and these must be replaced to ensure normal body functions. It is clear that normal diets based on 'straights', such as oats and hay, require supplementation with electrolytes.

Electrolyte Supplements

Assuming the basic diet is balanced with respect to electrolytes then a polo pony losing 5 litres (2 gallons) of sweat would require at least 10, 5 and 20g (0.35, 0.17 and 0.7oz) of sodium, potassium and chloride. (This assumes half the concentrations of electrolytes in the sweat stated previously.) It is advised that most electrolyte preparations are supplied in one dose per day, either in feed or in water.

At the time of writing (1996), it would seem that legislation may shortly prevent the sale of electrolyte mixtures, and this will mean that those responsible for feeding horses that sweat a lot will have to take great care to ensure that the appropriate elements are included in the feed.

HOT WEATHER/CLIMATES

The horse is a warm-blooded animal, and so he must keep his body temperature within the normal range under a wide range of different climates. These may vary from the very cold (–20°C/–4°F) to the very hot (40°C/104°F). Body temperature changes of 3°C (8°F) can result in death. Animals have what is called a 'zone of thermal neutrality', which is a temperature range in which they can easily maintain their proper body temperature. Below this range, the horse must increase heat production to stay warm and, above it, he must increase it in order to lose it and cool the body.

The zone of thermal neutrality may be as wide as 0–30°C (32–86°F), although it will vary between animals. Furthermore, it will be affected by body fat (especially subcutaneous fat), thickness of the coat and environmental factors, such as rain, wind, and so on. The general effect of environmental temperature on heat production is represented in Fig 28. It will be

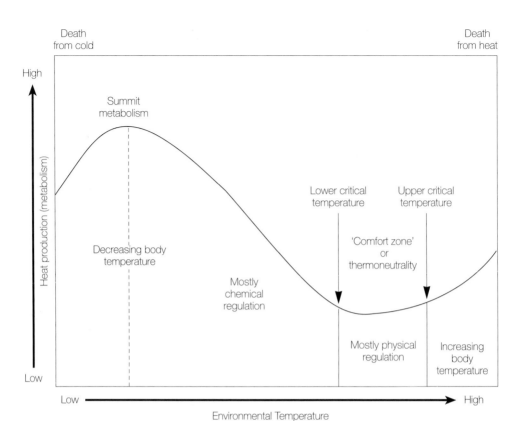

Death from cold

Death from heat

High

Heat production (metabolism)

Summit metabolism

Lower critical temperature

Upper critical temperature

Decreasing body temperature

'Comfort zone' or thermoneutrality

Mostly chemical regulation

Mostly physical regulation

Increasing body temperature

Low

Low

High

Environmental Temperature

Fig 28 Effect of environmental temperature on heat production.

apparent that at high environmental temperature (above the upper critical temperature) the temperature of the horse's body begins to increase. The horse loses heat to the environment in four ways:

- radiation
- convection
- evaporation
- conduction

The latter is of little significance since the surface area in contact with the ground is minimal, especially as the horse rests mostly in the standing position. When heat stress is not a problem, most heat is lost through radiation, convection and evaporation via the lungs. As the heat load increases through absorbed radiation from the sun, increased environmental temperature, heat production within the body during work, or by other means, sweating becomes the most important cooling mechanism available to the horse. Evaporative cooling mediated by sweat production accounts for only about 35 per cent of heat loss at 29°C (84°F), but almost 100 per cent at 36°C (97°F). (*See* Fig 29.)

Factors Affecting the Heat Load

Increases in the heat load as a result of high ambient temperatures cannot be prevented, and the effect of absorbed radiation from the sun can be minimized only

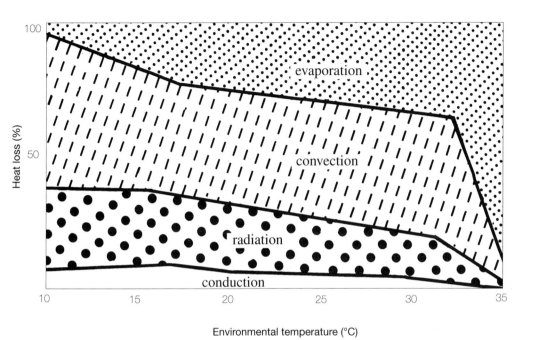

Fig 29 Effect of environmental temperature on proportional heat loss by different means.

by the provision of shade. The factor that is most amenable to manipulation is the heat production within the horse, and this is ameliorated via the feeding programme.

Food energy (gross energy) consumed by the horse is separated into that which is digested (digestible energy) and that which passes out of the body undigested. The quality of the feed (the fibre content) affects how much of the energy is digested: the energy digestibility of cereals varies between 70 and 90 per cent, and that of roughages between 30 and 60 per cent. Mixtures of cereal and roughage would have an energy digestibility of around 60 per cent. It is is estimated that 87–90 per cent of this digestible energy is metabolizable (available to the horse) and the rest – 10–13 per

cent – is 'wasted', excreted in the urine as nitrogen, or as gases (such as methane or hydrogen). The metabolizable energy can be divided into two categories: the net energy, which is that portion directly converted to maintenance of the body processes and work; and heat increment, which is the portion lost as heat during the process of digestion and nutrient utilization by the horse. This proportion of the metabolizable energy that is 'lost' as the heat increment is of crucial importance to the competition horse. Fig 30 shows how energy is metabolized in a horse fed a mixed diet of roughage and concentrate. Since the exact partition of energy losses depends on the precise source of the energy, it is shown to vary between two dotted lines.

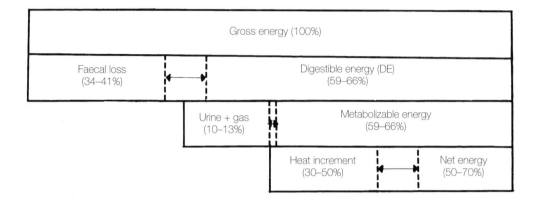

Fig 30 Energy metabolism in the horse.

Metabolizable energy used for maintenance is mostly converted to heat, apart from a small amount which is used by the horse when eating or moving around. The energy used for voluntary movement varies a lot between individual horses, and it has been suggested that this may in part account for the differences between good and poor doers.

When fed a mixed ration, it is estimated that 82 per cent of the food's metabolizable energy is used for maintenance and given off as heat energy, leaving about 18 per cent to be used for moving, eating, and so on. If we consider the metabolizable energy that is required for work, we find that in the horse the efficiency of converting food energy to work is very low, only about 20 per cent. This means that 80 per cent of the food energy available for work is wasted as heat (heat increment), and this heat is added to that released for maintenance. Clearly, the heat increment can have a considerable effect on the heat load that the working horse has to

expel. So it is important to know how it can be reduced.

Factors Affecting Heat Increment

ENERGY SOURCE
The heat increment of roughages is higher than that of cereals: 20 to 40 per cent of the food metabolizable energy compared to 5 to 10 per cent. The reason for this lies in the quantity of fibre contained within the foodstuff and thus there can be large differences, even between cereals. For example, the heat increment is higher when oats are fed than when maize is fed because the latter contains very little fibre.

NUTRIENT SOURCE
Carbohydrates are the primary sources of energy in a horse's diet, although more recently it has been shown that fats play a significant role and contribute to the reduction of heat production. The efficiency of utilization of these energy sources is reduced (thereby increasing heat production) when

protein is deficient. Conversely, excess protein can lead to large heat losses (+ 30 per cent) because of the energy required to remove waste nitrogen.

Feeding Strategies

The ingredients used in horse rations can be categorized according to their proportion of heat increment to metabolizable energy. Included in the lowest category are maize, barley, fats and oil; in an intermediate category are oats, soya and molasses; in the highest category are the high-fibre feeds, such as bran, and the roughages, such as hay.

When low heat increment feeds are provided, the total ration must be reduced because these feeds are also energy dense. Restriction of feed intake can create behavioural problems in horses unless they are very tired and content to rest during what would be 'normal feeding time'. Theoretically, a mix of maize and soya would meet the energy and protein requirements of the horse, but it would also be likely to cause digestive disturbances. A high-performance horse ration of oats and minimum intakes of hay could be improved by replacing the oats with maize and reducing feed intake (a reduction in oat intake and an increase in hay intake would obviously reduce the benefit to the horse).

An optimum ration for work in hot climates would include minimum roughage levels and mixed cereals. It is generally considered that a minimum roughage intake would be 500g (1.1lb) for every 100kg (220lb) of liveweight, and that total intake of food would be between 2 and 2.5kg (4.4–5.5lb) per 100kg. So a horse in full work could receive up to 2kg (4.4lb) of cereal per 100kg (220lb) of liveweight. The higher the energy density of the cereal mixture (more maize and oil) the lower the heat increment and the greater the risk of gut dysfunction. A compromise that is used successfully is a concentrate composed of equal parts oats and maize that may be top-dressed with oil (up to 10 per cent of the concentrate). Fats and oils can be used in place of molasses to 'bind' the ration together and hold in any dust. Salt should be included at 1 per cent of the concentrate.

Timing of Heat Production

Since fibrous feeds are associated with a large heat increment, they should be fed in the evening when no work is planned and the feed-related heat is produced during the coolest hours.

Heat production arising through maintenance functions are usually of a low level (about 2 MJ per hour for a 500kg/10cwt horse) over a 24-hour period. If the horse is working at the upper critical temperature, he will have to lose the additional heat of one hour's medium work by sweating. One gram (0.035oz) of sweat leads to the loss of 2.4kJ of heat, so the extra heat load of 16 MJ would require the evaporation of 6.7 litres (11.8 pints) of sweat! Fluid loss would be greater since some of the sweat would run off the horse's body before it could be evaporated to give the cooling effect. The sweat loss would contain electrolytes, which would have to be replaced in both the feed and the water. Clearly, work should be scheduled to occur at the coolest time of the day in order to minimize the heat load.

PRACTICAL FEEDING

Physical exercise is simply the conversion of energy into various forms and intensities of activity. So the nutritional needs of the performance horse are:

1. The energy required to support activity.
2. The nutrients needed for biochemical conversion of energy into muscular work.
3. The energy required to maintain the horse's body in the work performed.

Energy reserves and their rate of mobilization determine both the amount and speed of work that can be performed. The ration is the ultimate supplier of energy, and while the free-living horse is able to maintain an energy intake appropriate to his activity level, the 'modern' performance horse, enduring a heavy workload, is dependent on a well thought out feeding programme. The adequacy of the energy intake will be reflected in weight loss or gain.

It is essential to provide *clean* feed to performance horses. Ingestion of contaminated feed can give rise to a number of problems that will affect performance. Exercising horses need both roughage and concentrate. Roughage is essential to maintain the function of the gut and to provide the horse with something to occupy his time.

Summary Points

- The physically active performance horse shows very little additional need for protein, calcium, phosphorus, some of the trace minerals, and vitamins A, D and K. In contrast, there is a marked increase in the need for energy, electrolytes, vitamin E and the B-complex vitamins.
- There are no guaranteed supplements for general use; if there were, everybody would use them and the benefit would be lost. So effort is better directed towards providing a balanced ration.

Feeding recommendations

- Maximize low heat increment cereals (e.g. maize).
- Minimize roughage levels.
- Feed fibre-rich feeds during the coolest part of the day and when humidity is lowest.
- Feed little and often to spread heat load.
- Adjust feed intake to avoid overfeeding energy (minimize subcutaneous fat deposits).
- Feed fat or oil.
- Optimize protein intake.
- Balance ration to optimize electrolyte intake, particularly salt and potassium. (N.B. Salt and potassium are low in low-roughage diets.)
- Increase vitamin A, C and B complex levels.
- Check essential nutrient densities in view of the increased energy density of the ration and thus the lowered total intake of nutrients.
- Always provide plenty of fresh water and, ideally, accustom horses to drinking electrolyte mixtures.
- Always ensure feed is clean.

13

CLINICAL NUTRITION & FEED-RELATED PROBLEMS

Horses spend most of their 'active time' eating, the main drive being to maintain energy balance and thus survive. Ideally, energy intake should equal output, and failure to achieve this results in either obesity or weight loss. What signals the horse to seek and consume food remains as yet unknown, although we do know that temperature, glucose metabolism, body fat stores and other factors are involved in regulating food intake.

Temperature: Feed intake varies according to environmental temperature, so more time is spent eating when it is cold than when it is hot. Body temperature must be maintained despite heat loss. In addition, in hot weather horses seek shade and reduce their food intake thereby minimizing the food energy that must be dispersed.

Glucose: In contrast to the temperature control mechanism which can both increase and reduce food intake by the horse, the brain glucose mechanism works only one way: low brain glucose utilization stimulates feeding but high utilization rates do not suppress feeding activity.

Body fat stores: Assuming the horse has access to naturally growing foodstuffs, principally grass, then weight is gained during periods of plenty and lost when food is in short supply.

Other regulating factors: These may include things such as a short fast, followed by the provision of food which results in an immediate feeding response, recovery from illness and so on.

INAPPETANCE

Poor feeders can be a great worry. While there are drugs such as valium that can act as appetite stimulants, there are more preferable means of encouraging intake. Feeding within a group is known to work, and a feeding horse will encourage others. Turning horses out as opposed to stabling them may encourage eating. Adding succulents to the feed may also tempt a poor eater, as may adding sugar to the feed in the form of molasses; and in general coarse mixes are more palatable than pelleted compounds.

DIGESTIVE DISORDERS

These may be many and varied; however, they are usually strongly associated with feeding practices. Stabled horses kept for performance and leisure activities are at greatest risk when fed infrequent meals which are high in energy and low in forage, with limited free access to hay or grazing. Thus the establishment of a continuous feeding programme should be a priority in a stable where horses suffer from digestive disorders.

OLDER HORSES AND PONIES

Old horses are more likely to have dental disorders, and these can include loss of teeth, badly worn teeth, unevenly worn teeth and misalignment. The overall consequence of these problems is that the physical breakdown of long roughage is severely impaired. This may result in the horse swallowing large pieces of whole fibre or spending a much longer time eating. Large fibre pieces can accumulate and contribute to

impaction colic under conditions of impaired fibre digestion. Where the horse's teeth are ineffective in processing long fibre then it will be beneficial to provide soft food; a good example is soaked beet pulp which contains a lot of energy and highly digestible fibre. Another approach is to use processed fibre such as that found in dried grass/alfalfa cubes. These cubes may be soaked to provide a palatable, easily consumed, nutrient-rich feed.

There are various other problems from which the older horse can suffer, although there is very little detailed work on the specific needs of the geriatric horse. Common sense and an appreciation of the normal changes that occur during the ageing process enable the formulation of some simple guidelines:

1. Pay particular attention to dental care.
2. Be prepared to use 'special' foods if teeth are in bad shape.
3. Effectively control internal parasites.
4. Regulate the use of high fibre foods.
5. Be aware of competitive feeding situations within a group of horses.
6. Monitor liveweight constantly as a reflection of adequate energy intake.
7. Provide clean food.
8. Provide quality food.
9. Provide a balance of nutrients.
10. Keep the horse active.

TOO FAT OR TOO THIN?

Unfortunately, the assessment of body condition is very subjective and while numerous books and articles give guidelines on condition scoring, interpretation is inevitably variable: one person's idea of a condition score 5 might be another's 6. Most people's perception of well-being – of good condition – is synonymous with fatness. Generally, fatness is more acceptable than thinness in an animal because the latter implies lack of care. Owners of 'poor doers' are usually desperate to find a remedy and will often go to inordinate lengths to solve the 'problem'. So, while it might be very useful to define an optimum condition, it would be impossible to get a consensus on what precisely this should be.

However, we all have experience of horses or ponies that do very well on very little (good doers) and those that are difficult to put condition on. Both groups of animals can cause their owners considerable concern about how best they should be managed.

Underweight Animals

First it must be established that the animal's lack of condition is not caused by some underlying disease process, so your veterinary surgeon should be consulted. For example, there are many owners who may consider their worming programmes to be quite adequate, but on closer investigation it can be ascertained that they are not; and parasites are a common cause of poor body condition. It is important that the worming programme is developed *with* the veterinary surgeon to ensure that parasite control is adequate.

There are, of course, other conditions that can lead to chronic weight loss, and these must also be eliminated. Particularly difficult cases might involve those in

---

Parasites

Arthropods, controlled with insecticides

Lice	Mites
Biting midges	Warble fly
Botfly	Ticks

Worms, controlled with anthelmintics

Lungworm	Liver fluke

Gastrointestinal worms:
  Redworm (strongyles)
  Roundworm (ascarids)
  Threadworm (*Strongyloides westerii*)

---

which an animal has ostensibly recovered from a condition but has nevertheless sustained lasting damage. For example, such an animal might at some stage in his life have been heavily infested with parasites, during which period lasting damage was caused. Worms travelling through the blood vessels can cause parts of the gut to be 'starved' of blood, which may then render these parts only part-functional, or in more extreme cases completely non-functional. The net result is that the overall digestive and absorptive efficiency of the gut is reduced, and a horse so affected will get less benefit from his feed than another given the same diet.

Other types of 'hidden' damage might include impaired liver function following a bout of sub-acute ragwort poisoning; arthritic conditions might also play a part if the horse cannot move about and therefore graze freely. No one has quantified the effect of chronic pain on the horse's ability to maintain condition.

Abnormal behaviours, such as crib-biting, wind-sucking and weaving, can have an effect on the horse's ability to maintain weight. Weavers, for example, will indulge in prolonged periods of activity which can become quite frenetic. In order to maintain such activity the horse will draw on his food energy reserves, and this will probably not have been accounted for in his ration. Furthermore, when the horse is indulging in such behaviours, he is not eating, and so he is effectively reducing his intake; and the swallowing of air during windsucking might create a feeling of fulness which reduces the drive to eat. In the case of wind-sucking, it is considered that swallowing air might also lead to spasmodic colic, which in turn could reduce food intake.

Temperament is also a consideration. Flighty, active horses will use up more energy than placid animals, a difference in energy requirements that might be as great as 10 per cent either way. Thus, it follows that a highly strung horse will require more food to maintain condition than one who has a quiet nature.

Some horses that are difficult to keep in good condition have physical deformities that severely limit their ability to deal with roughages. An obvious example is the condition known as 'parrot-mouth', which makes it difficult for the horse to graze short grass. Equally, a horse with 'wave-mouth' would be unable effectively to grind his food prior to swallowing. Malocclusion of the teeth has been shown to result in a large increase (up to 50 per cent) in the number of chewing movements necessary to grind a kilo of roughage. So it is apparent that bodily condition is to some extent dependent on good dental care.

Having eliminated physical illness, deformity and abnormal behaviours as contributory factors, the obvious question is whether or not the horse is actually being fed enough, or ultimately receiving enough. The latter is especially relevant in a group feeding situation, in which shy feeders might be continually driven away by more dominant ones.

Assuming that a horse's energy needs have been properly assessed and catered for, and that all other possible physical factors have been eliminated, the first thing to do for an animal in poor condition is to reduce heat loss, particularly if the horse is outwintered. The most effective way of doing this is to provide rugs and shelter, although the benefit of the latter may be reduced if the animal is sharing it with more dominant animals. Having minimized heat loss, the following nutritional strategy should be followed:

1. Improve the quality of the basal roughage, either by substituting a leafy, rye-grass hay or by adding alfalfa to the existing roughage, making sure that the food is genuinely available *ad libitum*.

2. Add high-energy fibre sources. The most obvious would be soaked (for one hour) sugar beet shreds. If pellets are used, soaking time must be increased to four to five hours.

3. Feed processed roughage. Grass or alfalfa nuts contain roughage that has been ground prior to pelleting. They can be fed dry, but, if so, they must be 3–4mm in diameter. Larger pellets must

be soaked for four hours (1kg of pellets to 3 litres of water).

4. Soak roughage. Duration of soaking depends on the density of packing, but usually not more than one hour.

5. Add vegetable oil. Vegetable oil is energy dense, so a little has a large effect: 300g (10.5oz) contains the same energy as 1kg (2.2lb) of oats.

6. Use cooked cereals. These are more digestible than raw cereals.

7. Alter the forage–concentrate ratio. Although it is preferable to increase the energy intake by improving the quality of the raw materials in the diet, it may ultimately be necessary to feed more concentrate and less roughage.

Overweight Animals

Certain breed types are more prone to weight gain than others. Native ponies and cobs are good examples. Having adapted to exist in a fairly harsh environment in which they are obliged to travel long distances in search of food and water, the domesticated native pony is locked up in a small paddock or stable and provided with food on demand. The metabolism of these animals is geared to the storage of excess food energy as fat, the most obvious being subcutaneous fat. A Thoroughbred, on the other hand, is adapted for speed, where the energy is stored – initially at least – as glycogen in the liver and muscle.

The native pony needs to conserve energy for the times when food is scarce, and, in combination with a heavy coat, these fat reserves also act as an insulating layer to reduce heat loss and protect the animal from the elements. Other animals that are easy to overfeed are those that have a placid temperament, and these will include the warmblood types as well as the heavier horses.

The most obvious way to manage an overweight animal is to reduce his daily ration and thereby not satisfy his appetite and his motivation to feed. On the grounds of welfare, this is unacceptable because the animal should always have access to food. If quantity is not to be restricted then it follows that the quality of the diet must be changed. The type of diet fed will dictate the most appropriate strategy. For example, if the horse is fed roughage and concentrate, reduce or remove the latter from his diet. If only roughage is fed, dilute it with poorer (lower-energy) materials. The overall aim must be to reduce the energy intake while maintaining the intake of other nutrients necessary to assure good health. A simple idea to adopt is to make the horse work for his food by feeding him hay in a haynet with very small holes; and, at grass, by grazing the pasture first with sheep so that the horse subsequently has to work to obtain every blade of grass.

An appropriate nutritional strategy is as follows:

1. Confirm ration adequacy. Many people unwittingly overfeed, or feed concentrates unnecessarily. If you must feed concentrate, reduce the quality by using raw cereal instead of cooked, and use Horse and Pony cubes rather than competition mix.

2. Eliminate concentrates. Many animals will work off roughage and simply do not need any concentrate at all. And it is

surprising how much work they can do on such a diet. Remember that given his natural range in an undomesticated environment, a horse or pony could cover many miles a day without the need for any additive to his natural diet.

3. Reduce roughage quality. Use stemmy hay and/or substitute some good-quality barley or oat straw for some of the hay ration in order to reduce energy intake. However, remember that the demand for other nutrients remains, so feed a broad-spectrum supplement or a small amount of balancer that contains protein if protein is likely to be in short supply.

4. Work the animal. Placid animals by their very nature are inactive, so have someone exercise the horse, or put him on a horsewalker. Exercise is useful not only in that it burns off some of the excess energy, but in that it prevents the horse from eating!

5. Provide weather protection. Natural weather protection – the horse's natural winter coat, etc. – must be available to all animals, but do not overprotect him from the elements.

Whilst there are more factors to consider when dealing with the horse in poor condition, the overweight animal is probably more difficult to manage because it can be very difficult to separate our personal need to be generous from the necessity to control the qualitative intake of the horse. However, once the various points are appreciated, it should be fairly easy to develop a logical strategy to suit any horse's needs and condition.

STABLED HORSES

Stable vices include behaviours such as crib-biting, wind-sucking, weaving, box-walking and self-mutilation, and are described by scientists as stereotypies. The name 'stable vice' indicates that the behaviour develops when horses are stabled and are rarely reported in horses that have never been stabled. The use of the word 'vice' is incorrect since it is not the horse that is at fault, but rather the circumstances in which it is kept.

There are various myths associated with this problem and it is important to realize that stable vices are not:
- bad behaviour
- copied or learned
- caused by boredom
- caused by lack of space
- incurable

So the question remains, what are stable vices and how do they develop? Stabled horses are unable to perform their full, natural repertoire of behaviour because they may be confined, isolated from other horses, and fed 'unnatural' feed in an 'unnatural' way. The horse finds this frustrating and, as a result, some individuals may develop a stereotypic behaviour which we believe helps that particular animal to cope with its environment.

If all stabled horses are frustrated then why do they not all develop stable vices? Some horses are more sensitive than others to their surroundings in the same way that some people are less tolerant than others. Differences between people and between horses are owed in part to the differences in the complex nerve cells in certain parts of the brain that are inherited from the parents. Chemical substances are produced which act in these cells – more sensitive animals have more cells, are more reactive and may develop a vice. The animal simply cannot help it! If both parents have stereotypies then there is a very high risk (odds of 9:10) that the foal will react to frustration in the same way; remember the foal does not copy or mimic the mare's 'bad' behaviour. If both parents are free of stereotypies but the grandparents or other offspring have stable vices then the odds are about 1:4. Approximately 8 per cent of all horses show some stereotypic behaviour.

It is difficult to understand how apparently well-looked after horses and ponies can be frustrated. But in even the best-kept yards there are two features which can make the stable environment less than ideal:
1. Less than 12 hours' feeding time.
2. Lack of complete social contact with other horses.

Horses naturally feed for up to seventeen hours a day and are herd animals forming natural groupings of between six and ten. Seeing and sniffing other horses over a partition or through bars is not enough social contact. Horses may become aroused through disturbances or excitement in the yard; the arrival of new horses, for example, would be highly stimulatory. Susceptible horses aroused in this way may then perform vices. Other triggering factors include sudden isolation, illness, injury and the provision of food. Excitement results in the release of a substance known as beta-endorphin which stimulates some of the nerve cells; in those animals that have more cells the process leads to the performance of a stereotypic behaviour or stable vice.

Treatment for Stable Vices

Traditionally, treatments for vices have included physical methods of preventing the animal from performing the behaviour: using crib straps, grills and even surgical intervention. These methods are not particularly successful. For example, weavers whose doors have been fitted with anti-weave bars continue to weave by simply stepping back from the door. It has been estimated that 80 per cent of horses that have had surgery to the strap muscle can – and do – still wind-suck. Obviously, prevention of the behaviour by physical means increases the level of frustration and reduces the welfare of the animal still further.

Colic is often considered to be a sequel to wind-sucking. However, it is possible that underlying digestive disorders may predispose the horse to wind-suck, thus aggravating the whole situation. The use of a flute bit may be useful in this case since it allows the horse to perform the behaviour but stops the animal swallowing air. Crib-biting results in incisor wear and, sometimes, chipping of the teeth. Excessive wear (down to the gums!) can be prevented by making a 'comforter' available to the horse. This is something the horse can crib on yet will not damage the teeth. Manger rims, tops of bars and ledges can be covered with yielding, yet hard-wearing, materials – tyre rubber or coconut matting are possibilities. Alternatively, a vulcanite bit can be used. Horses that persist in crib-biting when at grass can ruin fence lines, so the provision of a large post at chest height that is covered with the appropriate material can prevent untoward damage. The use of these devices for cribbing purposes can be encouraged by liberally smearing them with treacle or molasses while the horse is held in close proximity.

The provision of alternative activities can 'use up' spare time that might be spent performing stereotypies. Obviously, turn out onto pasture with other horses will encourage free movement, social interaction as well as grazing activity. However, this simple solution is not always possible, particularly for those horses in hard work. So, if the work period can be extended, particularly in the company of other horses, this will ease the problem and reduce frustration. Horse-walkers are particularly useful in this context since it is possible to gently exercise four to six horses simultaneously for extended periods of time.

Horse cribbing on fence post.

Depending on the work required, it may be possible to increase the roughage allowance and thereby extend the feeding time. Animals in hard work will have a limited roughage allocation, so alternative means of extending feeding time have to be used. Accessibility of the roughage may be reduced by using small-holed haynets, or a number of conventional haynets inside one another, or by suspending a number of small haynets around the stable to encourage the horse to move around and to be selective. Another approach is to mix different forages to encourage selective feeding behaviour thereby slowing down the rate of intake. Concentrate consumption rates can be reduced by sprinkling the hard feed over roughage so that it has to be picked out, and putting large, *smooth* stones in the manger means that the animal has to push them around to get at food.

Loose-housing works very well with groups of horses, provided care is taken to introduce horses properly to the group and to watch out for bullies. This system of housing allows animals to move around freely, interact more, and generally provides a more natural way of life which is less frustrating for the horse. Animals should be bedded generously with straw and several feeding points established. The latter prevents competition or bullying and animals can wander about from point to point. Big round bales are ideal in this environment since the horses can help themselves on an *ad lib* basis and food is available twenty-four hours every day. Equally, there should be several watering points at different locations.

It is important to realize that changing the management of horses will not suddenly lead to the disappearance of stable vices: they often take a long time to develop so it is not unexpected that they can take a long time to disappear. Susceptible horses are usually both more alert and active, and they learn more quickly than others. Once these individuals are recognized then they should be managed with extra care, taking into account the above points in order to minimize the risk of their developing stereotypies.

AZOTURIA

The term 'azoturia' frequently causes some confusion in that it is often used with reference to another separate condition, which has similar symptoms but occurs at a different time and for different reasons.

The condition known as 'tying up', 'myositis' or 'setfast' is different to and less severe than azoturia. Tying up occurs after work when the burning up of muscle energy reserves (glycogen) has led to the accumulation of lactic acid in the muscles. The result is stiffness and obvious dis comfort. In contrast, azoturia, also known as exertional rhabdomyolysis, occurs at the beginning of exercise. In days gone by it was known as 'Monday morning disease' because it occurred in draught horses when they were put back to work after a

weekend's inactivity during which they continued to receive full rations. This is the key to understanding the major cause of azoturia, which lies in feeding mismanagement although, of course, it is important that horses are 'warmed up' properly prior to work. An inadequate warm-up period can exacerbate azoturia, as well as predispose the horse to muscle strain.

There are two important aspects of feeding management that can increase the likelihood of azoturia occurring. The first and most obvious is the failure to tailor the quantity of food given to the energy required for the work performed; the second is a mineral imbalance, which can also lead to muscle dysfunction.

Food Intake

The draught horses that were maintained on full rations over the weekend might have consumed 9–10kg (20–22lb) of cereal daily. While the animal was at rest, the cereal would be digested and glucose produced, which would then be absorbed and converted to glycogen, and then stored in large quantities in the liver and muscles. The resumption of work on Monday morning would initiate the mobilization of these glycogen reserves, which results in the accumulation of breakdown products (mainly lactic acid). These products make the muscles very acid, which in turn damages muscle protein. This causes the release of myoglobin, which appears in the urine and reddens it. The muscle damage is extremely painful. Racehorses, and other horses, fed large amounts of cereal when not working can experience the same problem.

It will be apparent from this that prevention is easily achieved by drastically cutting back the concentrate allowance when the horse is not working, and allowing adequate warm-up prior to the reintroduction of work. It is also worth pointing out that it is beneficial to the horse if he 'warms down' after hard work: this facilitates lactic acid removal from the muscles, and may take the form of cantering, followed by trotting and then walking.

MINERAL IMBALANCE
Most diets based on the feeding of hay and oats are grossly imbalanced with respect to minerals. In his natural environment, the horse would not work, and all his mineral needs would be met by the grass (*see* Table 13.1). However, horses in hard work require more energy, and to provide it we need to replace some of the roughage with concentrate. If straight cereals, such as oats, are used then the mineral profile of the ration is affected because oats have a completely different profile from grass: for example, oats have only 10 per cent of the sodium content of grass. This is best illustrated in Table 13.1, which shows a significant shortage of sodium in horses that are in medium work and fed hay and oats. With those horses in hard work, the problem is exacerbated because large quantities of sodium are lost in sweat.

Concentrate feeding also affects calcium balance. Concentrates contain large amounts of phosphorus, and this adversely

Table 13.1 A comparison of the minerals supplied (g per day) with the minerals required (shown in brackets) by a 500kg horse resting, in moderate work and in hard work

	Resting (at grass)	Moderate work	Hard work
Ration:	35kg	7kg hay + 4kg oats	5kg hay + 8.5kg oats
Minerals:			
Calcium	41 (28)	37 (42)	30 (58)
Phosphorus	16 (14)	29 (21)	38 (29)
Magnesium	13 (8)	16 (11)	17 (15)
Sodium	13 (8)	14 (28)	11 (35)
Potassium	229 (25)	139 (37)	127 (50)
Supplements:			
Salt	–	33	60
Limestone	–	33	48
(Alfalfa)	–	(700)	(1,000)

affects the calcium–phosphorus ratio. Calcium needs to be added to the diet to ensure the correct calcium–phosphorus ratio of 2:1. Also, in concentrate-rich diets, magnesium supplies are marginal. These minerals are essential for normal neuromuscular function and a deficiency may result in azoturia. So the horse that is in hard work and fed only hay and cereal requires large quantities of salt and calcium to rectify the mineral imbalances. Limestone is a cheap source of calcium, but is unpalatable, and also tends to separate out from the other feed ingredients. A plant source of calcium is alfalfa/lucerne: 1kg (2.2lb) of alfalfa will supply about 18g (0.6oz) of calcium, which is the equivalent to a supplement of some 50g (1.8oz) of limestone. So, as shown in Table 13.1, a calcium shortage could be rectified by feeding alfalfa in place of hay 700g (1.4lb) for a horse in medium work; 1kg for the same horse in hard work.

The traditional system of feeding hay and oats is favoured by some 80 per cent of racehorse trainers, in which case inadequate mineral supplementation will increase the likelihood of azoturia. Some trainers opt for a compromise by feeding a combination of oats and compounded concentrate; a few rely entirely on compounded products. Circumstantial evidence suggests that horses fed in this way are less susceptible to azoturia. The explanation lies in the fact that the mineral balance is much better in horses fed hay and compound (*see* Table 13.2). It is apparent that there is no need to supplement these rations, and that the mineral balance is suitable for the horse at different levels of work.

Although there are no reliable data to indicate which animals are particularly susceptible to azoturia, informed opinion is that fillies and mares in work seem to be more vulnerable than colts or geldings.

Table 13.2 A comparison of the minerals supplied (g/day) by rations based on compounds with the minerals required (shown in brackets) by a 500kg horse in moderate and hard work

Ration:	Moderate work 7kg hay + 4kg racing mix	Hard work 5kg hay + 8.5kg racing mix
Minerals:		
Calcium	83 (42)	127(58)
Phosphorus	41 (21)	63 (29)
Magnesium	22 (11)	28 (15)
Sodium	34 (28)	52 (35)
Potassium	179 (37)	212 (50)

This is probably because when fillies and mares are showing cyclical activity there are significant changes in circulating hormone levels. The sex hormones have been shown to be associated with those that affect mineral metabolism. It seems likely that around oestrus, mineral handling and thus mineral balance is upset, and those animals on marginal mineral intakes will be prone to azoturia. One way of dealing with this problem is to supply excess available calcium so that in spite of an altered efficiency in mineral handling the horse will have sufficient mineral reserves to support muscle function.

Comparison of blood mineral values with those in the urine can give some indication of the horse's mineral status, although urinary loss of minerals can be affected by the nature of the diet. This means that there can be difficulties in interpreting the results of the test, and so the best approach is undoubtedly one of prevention. To ensure that your horse receives an adequate supply, either check the mineral status of your horse's diet and provide the necessary supplements, or use a compounded product in place of straight cereal.

Azoturia is a problem created by us for our horses, so we should make every effort to ensure their welfare by making every attempt to get their diets right. This means feeding a balanced diet with quantities calculated according to work done.

LAMINITIS

Feed-related laminitis is the consequence of overfeeding carbohydrate, either as soluble carbohydrate in grass, or as storage polysaccharides (starch), which is typically found in cereals.

In simple terms, the pH (a measure of acidity/alkalinity) balance of the large intestine is affected by excess carbohydrate because substrates – which are normally digested in the small intestine – pass into the hind gut. Here they are rapidly fermented into acids (in particular lactic acid), which lowers (makes more acidic) the pH of the gut contents. When the gut environment's pH is low, many organisms die off, releasing their cell contents – including endotoxins – which cannot normally cause any harm to the host animal because they cannot normally escape from the cell. However, the death and rupturing of the cell means that these endotoxins are suddenly freed into the gut.

There are also enterotoxins, which, again, cause no harm in the healthy gut because they are contained by the gut wall. But when the gut contents become very acid, the gut wall becomes permeable to both endo- and enterotoxins. The passage of these toxins then stimulates a powerful inflammatory response which can ultimately lead to laminitis. During the process of aberrant fermentation within the large intestine, it is likely that the horse will also suffer some degree of colic.

Laminitis is obviously better prevented, and this can be achieved by controlling the consumption of carbohydrate. Horses should not be given large feeds of cereal, and the feeding routine should mimic the little-and-often trickle feeding that is observed in horses grazing in natural conditions. When at grass, horses and ponies should not suddenly be given access to lush, heavily fertilized swards. Horses that have been wintered in stables and then turned out to spring grass can consume large quantities of sugar-rich grass in a very short period of time. Those animals that are especially prone to laminitis (obese horses or ponies and native breeds), should have access only to tightly grazed swards where they have to 'work' for their grass.

Laminitis-prone horses present a real management problem because while it is relatively easy to control their intake of easily digestible material over the winter period, it is very different when they are at grass. Some strategies adopted by owners amount to chronic starvation, and therefore compromise the animal's welfare. Keeping him on concrete and limiting his access to grass ignores his behavioural need to eat for at least sixteen hours in every twenty-four. The key to success is rather to feed a low-energy diet that does not contain readily fermentable carbohydrates: high-fibre forages, such as timothy hay, and/or straw to which the animal can have continuous access. This can be provided in a ring-feeder in a paddock that has previously been grazed bare by other herbivores, so that the pony or horse has to search hard for grass and, because it will be very short, the rate of consumption will be slow.

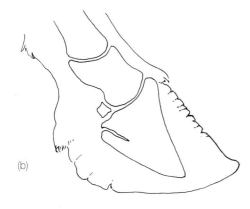

Fig 31 The laminitic foot: showing (a) elongation of the toe and the characteristic rings that appear on the coronet and progress downwards as the horn grows; and (b) rotation of the pedal bone, which occurs after separation of the horny and sensitive laminae in acute cases.

The Post-Laminitis Diet

A horse that has had laminitis will have suffered significant tissue damage and trauma, so to make a good recovery he needs good food. This is necessary to provide the nutrients to repair the damaged tissues and to meet the increased energy needs associated with the changes in metabolic rate that occur during such traumatic episodes. Traditionally, post-laminitic animals were put on poor quality diets of hay and bran, but fortunately this practice is dying out. The basis of the diet should be good-quality forage with low levels of *soluble* carbohydrate. Such diets can be 50:50 mixes of good quality forage (16 per cent protein) with timothy hay or oat straw (which provide plenty of carbohydrate, but in a complex fibre form which is slowly fermented). Good quality protein is vital to aid tissue repair, and must form a minimum of 8 per cent of the nutrient intake. Dehydrated forms of alfalfa and grass are good sources, and far preferable to straw, which contains protein but in a way that renders it less available to the horse.

COLIC

This condition occurs all too frequently and is a result of poor management; this means that most cases of colic are preventable. For many, colic is synonymous with a blockage in the animal's gut. However, in simple terms the word means abdominal pain and young children are often described as colicky when they suffer from persistent abdominal discomfort that arises from pressure exerted by gas that is 'trapped' in the gut. In the horse there are three easily recognized forms of colic:
• impaction colic
• sand colic
• gas colic

Impaction Colic

Impactions are blockages that occur somewhere in the gastrointestinal tract and prevent the movement of food residues. They usually occur at places where the lumen narrows or where there is a bend or twist, such as occurs at the flexures. It has been said that the horse's gut was designed by a committee whose members failed to talk to one another! Physically, it is not a well-designed tube, having several changes in internal diameter as well as direction. The closer the impaction to the anus the better since it is more accessible and treatable with enemas and so on. An impaction at the ileo-caecal junction is 'out of reach' and therefore more difficult to treat. Unless an impaction is cleared reasonably quickly, the animal may begin to dehydrate and if there is plenty of fermentable substrate around then more gas may be produced than can easily be got rid of. The general lack of movement of the gut under such conditions exacerbates the problem.

Impaction colics often occur when horses are fed high-fibre forages such as straw, or when there is an inadequate water intake, or when there has been a dramatic dietary change. All of these factors can cause the problem independently or in any combination. Thus, taking animals off grass, housing them, and then feeding them a poor quality timothy hay could easily create such a colic. Other factors may also contribute. Old horses in particular whose teeth are in poor condition cannot effectively chew high fibre feeds; and because of their age, they are more likely to have been exposed to worm damage. Parts of the gut can be permanently damaged and because of this may be less well supplied with blood, less 'mobile', and thus always a region more vulnerable to problems.

Sand Colic

Sand colic is associated with ingestion of sand either voluntarily or involuntarily. The latter can happen when animals are grazing on grass that is very short and growing on sandy soil in which the roots do not have a very good hold. So when the horse pulls at the grass, he will lift the whole plant, and consume it together with its sand-covered roots. This process of involuntary ingestion of soil can lead to very high intakes, at least a kilogram (2.2lb) per day. Sand is very dense and when it collects in the tract may lead to a colic.

Some horses voluntarily consume soil although we do not know why. Many people believe that the horse is 'nutritionally wise' and is seeking some specific nutrients; but while this may be true for salt there is no evidence to support this contention otherwise. If the horse persistently eats sand-rich soil he will be at risk. Prevention can only be achieved by moving the animal to another paddock or stabling him.

Gas Colic

Gas colic arises when animals have access to highly fermentable material in large quantities. In simple terms, when gas produced as a byproduct of fermentation cannot be removed quickly enough from the gut it 'blows up'. This can rupture the stomach characterized by the animal adopting a dog sitting pose. It has fatal consequences. Excess starch, such as in feeding ground maize meal, or excess soluble carbohydrate as in early season grass can cause such a problem.

Gas colic in the large intestine can occur through too much fermentable material being fed and escaping normal digestion in the small intestine. *Lactobacilli* can act very quickly on this type of material, producing gas as well as lactic acid, which can lead to laminitis as described previously. Thus care is needed in feeding high quality feeds; little and often is the golden rule which is unfortunately too often ignored.

Summary Points
- Good forage is the basis of good feeding.
- Progressive replacement of forage with concentrate can lead to problems.
- High levels of concentrate can encourage stereotypic behaviour and lead to colic and laminitis.
- Mineral imbalance occurs when horses are fed low levels of roughage.
- When concentrate feeding is necessary, care should be taken to balance the diet and feed little and often.
- Care of the teeth, especially in the older animal, is most important.

14

RATION FORMULATION

BASIS OF FEEDING SYSTEMS

Energy is required to maintain life and animals continuously respond to their energy intake. If horses are fed excess energy they become fat, and if they are not fed enough then they utilize body reserves and lose weight. In contrast, it is possible to double the vitamin or protein intake over a number of days with little apparent effect; doubling the energy intake of a horse over the same period would lead to weight increase and an unmanageable horse! Furthermore the bulk of any food or diet is composed of energy sources, the major one being carbohydrate. This can be in a complex form, as plant fibre, or as a storage polysaccharide such as starch or more simply as soluble carbohydrate. Because of the foregoing, animals are rationed on the basis of energy, so the starting point for working out diets for horses is to determine their energy needs.

ENERGY FOR MAINTENANCE

The energy needs of an animal depend primarily on body size (weight in kg) and secondly on physiological status (pregnant, lactating or working). For those animals at rest (maintenance) it is a relatively easy matter to determine their energy requirements. For example to determine the requirements of a 500kg horse at maintenance:

digestible energy (DE) requirements (MJ/day) = $4.184 (1.4 + 0.03 \times$ liveweight in kg)

so

$$DE \text{ (MJ/day)} = 4.184 (1.4 + 0.03 \times 500)$$
$$= 4.184 (1.4 + 15)$$
$$= 4.184 \times 16.4$$
$$= 68.6$$

Clearly, all you need to know is the horse's weight, which can be determined fairly easily by using:

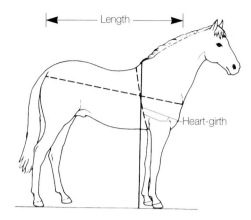

Fig 32 The formula for calculating a horse's weight using heart-girth and length measurements will not be quite as accurate as the weigh-tape method.

1. A weightape;
2. A weighbridge;
3. An equation.

Examples of suitable equations are:

1. Weight (kg) = $\dfrac{\text{girth (cm}^2) \times \text{length (cm)}}{11{,}900}$

(length$_{cm}$ = point of shoulder to point of buttocks [tuber ischii])

2. Weight (kg) = $\dfrac{[\text{umbilical girth (cm)}]^{1.78} \times [\text{length (cm)}]^{0.97}}{3011}$

(length$_{cm}$ = elbow to point of buttocks (tuber ischii)]

Thus, the minimum equipment required to estimate the weight of a horse or pony is a measuring tape and a calculator. It is inadvisable to rely on condition scoring because it is very subjective and what is observed when scoring an animal is the result of previous energy intakes: a fat animal that scores highly tells you that past feeding was incorrect and, therefore, condition scoring measures history. Weight changes are more immediate and can tell you quickly if feeding is appropriate or in which way it should be changed.

Once you know the horse's energy requirement, in this case 68.6 MJ DE/day for a 500kg horse, all you have to do is find out what feeds are available, discover their energy content and make up a ration! We need to have some idea of likely food intake before we proceed and a useful 'rule of thumb' is 2 per cent of liveweight or 2kg of *dry feed* per 100kg liveweight.

So for a 500kg horse we would expect an intake of 10kg of dry feed such as hay.

The animal needs 68.6 MJ DE in 10kg, so the minimum energy concentration will be:

$$\frac{68.6\ \text{MJDE}}{10\text{kg dry feed}} = 6.86\ \text{MJDE/kg dry feed}$$

Straw has a DE less than 6 MJ per kg so, apart from other nutrient considerations, it could not supply enough energy. A leafy hay or legume, such as lucerne, with a DE of about 9 MJ per kg would easily supply the need within appetite:

$68.6 \div 9 = 7.6\text{kg of feed}$

The problem here is that if fed to appetite, the horse would consume more energy than he needs, i.e. if the horse eats 10kg of lucerne per day then he would consume 90 MJ DE per day, which is 1.31 times what he needs. This 40 per cent of extra energy would be likely to lead to over-fatness if feeding continued at this level. If good quality forage is all that is available then it can be diluted with oat straw or poor quality hay so that the appetite can be satisfied without overfeeding energy. If we have a high quality forage (9 MJ/kg) and a low quality forage (5 MJ/kg) then they can be blended together to produce a mix that will satisfy both energy and appetite requirements. We need to use a simple proportioning method called Pearson's Square. For this to work we need two feeds: one (B) with a value **less** than the desired specification and one (A) with a value **greater than** the specification. For example, the specification we need is the total energy requirement (68.6 MJ DE) divided by the estimated dry feed intake (10kg):

$$\frac{68.6}{10} = 6.86 \text{ MJ DE/kg dry feed.}$$

If we have two forages (A and B), one with a value of 9 MJ DE/kg(A) and the other with a value of 5 MJ DE/kg(B), we set out the square as follows:

Available forages	Specification	Desired proportions
A 9		▶ 1.86
B 5		▶ 2.14

To obtain the desired proportions we take the lesser value from the greater value **diagonally**. To convert these values to percentages we sum the proportion (1.86 + 2.14 = 4) and then express the proportion of each forage as a percentage of the total, i.e:

$$\frac{\text{percentage of}}{\text{A in mix}} = \frac{1.86}{4.00} \times 100 = 46.5\%$$

$$\frac{\text{percentage of}}{\text{B in mix}} = \frac{2.14}{4.00} \times 100 = 53.5\%$$

To be absolutely precise, we could multiply the percentages of each ingredient (A or B) by the expected dry food intake to find out how much of each forage to feed, i.e:

$$\text{A needed } \frac{46.5}{100} \times 10 = 4.65\text{kg of A}$$

$$\text{B needed } \frac{53.5}{100} \times 10 = 5.35\text{kg of B}$$

However, in practice this level of precision is both unnecessary and unrealistic, and since A is of better quality it is simpler to round up its value to 50 per cent and feed 5kg, and to reduce the value of B to 50 per cent and to feed 5kg. This will produce a simple 50:50 mix of roughage which will contain fractionally more energy than necessary, although in practice the effect on the animal will be minimal.

A major problem occurs if the horse under-eats, that is, eats less than the estimated 10kg of dry feed. If he is a fussy feeder and persistently leaves his feed, he will lose weight unless we adjust the forage proportions. If for example, the horse eats only 76 per cent of expected dry food intake (.76 × 10 = 7.6kg per day) then he would receive only 76 per cent of his energy requirement for maintenance. Failure to adjust the diet would lead to loss of weight. Recalculation for the reduced intake means that the requirement (68.6 MJ DE) would have to be contained in 7.6kg of dry feed, and thus the specified energy density of 6.86 MJ DE/kg would change to:

$$\frac{68.6}{7.6} = 9.0 \text{ MJ/kg dry feed}$$

Clearly, this value is equivalent to that of the best quality forage (A) and it would have to be fed by itself in order to meet energy needs. Intakes between 76 and 100 per cent of expected dry food intake would require that these two forages be re-proportioned according to a revised speci-fication, calculated from the maintenance requirement (68.6 MJ DE) and the actual intake (x kg), i.e.

$$\frac{68.6}{x} = \text{revised spec. MJ DE/kg dry feed}$$

Having done the calculations and worked out how much to feed, it is essential to mon-itor weight and dry feed intake to make sure the animal is neither gaining nor losing weight. If he gains, it is likely that he is eat-ing more than the calculated allowance and therefore the specification has to be reduced. Conversely, loss of weight indi-cates under-eating and the need to increase the energy density of the dry feed. If only poor quality roughage is available then it may be necessary to feed some concentrate alongside the roughage. A general rule of feeding is always to maximize the forage intake within the constraints of appetite.

Because of differences in temperament, calculated energy requirements can be wrong by + or –10 per cent, so always be prepared to adjust energy supplies and diets for individuals. The ability to do this reflects skill and is where the art of feed-ing comes in; scientific calculations can take you so far and, thereafter, personal judgement is required.

Environmental conditions can have a substantial effect on energy requirements and the smaller animal (assuming it **not** to be a native pony) is disadvantaged because *pro rata* he has a greater body surface to

weight ratio than the large horse, and there-fore is more vulnerable in terms of heat loss. Under adverse weather conditions (cold, wind and rain) requirements for maintenance can be increased by up to 40 per cent although the provision of shelter or a New Zealand rug can substantially reduce this need. A rug is the most effective way of limiting heat losses, making the animal more comfortable and saving on feed costs! Do not wait until the animal has lost weight before you feed more. If the weather is awful then rug the horse and feed him immediately, before he has to use up body reserves to keep warm. Good-quality roughage is the best feed for outwintered horses and is the foundation feed for any good ration. Concentrate usage is the last resort when either the forage is very poor, or the animal simply can't eat enough.

Since maintenance feeding depends so heavily on the use of forages it is essential that they are of the best hygienic quality. This is critical for housed, sport horses

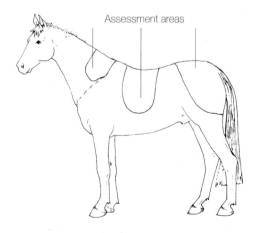

Fig 33 Condition scoring in the horse.

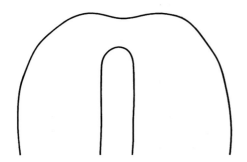

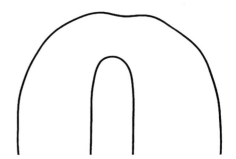

Fig 34 Condition score 5 – obese: very bulging rump; deep gutter along the back; ribs too buried to be felt; marked crest; folds and lumps of fat.

Fig 35 Condition score 4 – fat: rump too well rounded; gutter along the back; ribs and pelvis difficult to feel.

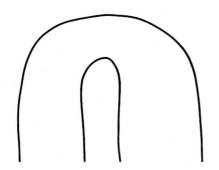

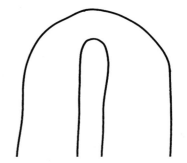

Fig 36 Condition score 3 – good: rump rounded; ribs covered but easy to feel; neck firm, no crest.

Fig 37 Condition score 2 – thin: rump flat either side of backbone; ribs visible; narrow but firm neck.

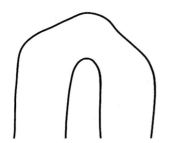

Fig 38 Condition score 1 – poor: rump sunken; cavity under tail; ribs prominent; backbone and croup prominent; ewe neck, narrow and slack.

Fig 39 Condition score 0 – very poor: rump very sunken; deep cavity under tail; skin tight over prominent bones; backbone and pelvis very prominent; marked ewe neck, very narrow.

whose performance depends on healthy, 100 per cent lung function. It may be that hygienic quality has a lower priority for horses outside since respiratory allergens are more likely to be blown away than inhaled. Generally, nutritive value takes second place in the list of priorities since nutrients that are deficient in the forage can always be obtained from supplementary concentrates.

Large Horses (over 600kg) and Small Ponies (under 200kg)

These animals fall outside the 'normal range' and calculating the energy requirements for these two groups is fraught with difficulties. Small ponies include many native ponies which seem to do well on fresh air; that is, calculated requirements seem to exceed their need. Thus, caution must be exercised when rationing these animals and care taken not to overfeed. This requires constant and accurate monitoring of liveweight and if increases are seen then it is important to reduce the energy density/specification of the diet.

Generally, the larger horses are easier to deal with since, on the whole, they are less active than 'light' horses and therefore require proportionately less energy. You can use the same equation as shown above and then reduce the value obtained by between 10 and 15 per cent, i.e. multiply it by 0.9 to 0.85 to obtain a more realistic estimate of actual need. Using the 200–600kg equation would supply about 10.5 MJ DE too much to an 800kg heavy horse. However, multiplying the value by 0.9 gives the correct value.

Energy for Work

This is easily calculated because we can work in multiples of maintenance. For example, the horse in intense work will require about twice his maintenance need so for the 500kg horse in very hard work, $2 \times 68.6 = 137.2$ MJ DE will be required per day. The **big** problem is to decide the intensity of work between maintenance (M) and the highest level of work (2M). Obviously, medium work will be equivalent to $1.5 \times 68.6 = 102.9$ MJ DE per day. It is possible to devise a scale from 0 to 10 where 0 equals maintenance (M) and 10 is equal to 2M. Work rates in between these extremes will be a value between 1 and 10 and for each unit the horse will need an additional $68.6 \div 10 = 6.86$ MJ DE. Thus a horse in light work (M + 3) will require M + (3 × 6.86) or 68.6 + (3 × 6.86) which is equal to 89.18 MJ DE.

Most people will overvalue the amount of work their horses are doing and as a consequence, overfeed them. In other words, a horse doing M + 3 work might be fed as if he were doing M + 5 work and receive an additional 13.72 MJ DE per day (equivalent to a kilogram of maize!). This is not a great problem if owners operate a strict and regular programme of weight calculation because this overfeeding will soon be picked up as an increase in liveweight. Of course the horse may also become unridable in the interim since he will not be doing enough work in relation to his energy intake. Another lesser problem is that once in work, some horses get more 'worked up' and require extra energy **above** their work requirement to replace that which is burned-off through over-excitement.

The initial stage for rationing a horse in hard work is to assess his energy need (2 × M) based on liveweight, look at the feeds available and make an estimate of intake. In the case of a 500kg horse, he will have to consume 137.2 MJ DE and likely intake will be 12/13kg of dry feed. Thus, the minimum energy density will be 137.2 ÷ 13 = 10.55 MJ DE/kg. If we have a leafy hay (8 MJ DE/kg) and oats (11.5 MJ kg) then we can balance them using Pearson's Square:

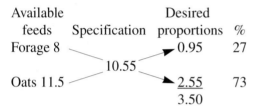

Available feeds	Specification	Desired proportions	%
Forage 8		➤ 0.95	27
	10.55		
Oats 11.5		➤ 2.55	73
		3.50	

This type of mix represents the most extreme of those used for racehorses since 27 per cent forage is equivalent to 3.5kg per day together with 9.5kg oats. Generally, we prefer to feed 1 per cent dry forage which is 1kg/100kg and in this case would be equivalent to 5kg per day so the above ration is 1.5kg low in long fibre. A better quality forage with a DE of 10 MJ/kg would have a very beneficial effect.

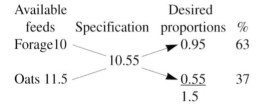

Available feeds	Specification	Desired proportions	%
Forage 10		➤ 0.95	63
	10.55		
Oats 11.5		➤ 0.55	37
		1.5	

Thus, a quality forage can have a large effect on forage/concentrate proportions and in this case, the horse could be fed

8.2kg forage and 4.8kg oats **assuming** he continued to eat his full ration of 13kg. But note that horses in work generally eat more than those at rest.

A problem that arises when feeding straight cereals is a serious deficiency of some nutrients. For example, a diet of forage and oats will not contain enough protein, calcium or sodium for horses in hard work. If we consider our 500kg horse in intense work, he will require 137.2 MJ DE per day (2 × 68.6). If we have a moderate hay (8 MJ DE/kg) and a cereal (12.5 MJ DE/kg) we can balance them to achieve the desired specification of 10.55 MJ DE/kg mix assuming an intake of 13kg of dry feed.

Available feeds	Specification	Desired proportions	%
Hay 8		➤ 1.95	43
	10.55		
Cereal 12.5		➤ 2.55	57
		4.5	

The actual amounts of feed in the ration will be 5.6kg hay (43/100 × 13) and 7.4kg cereal (57/100 × 13). The protein requirement is related to energy intake by the following:

$$\frac{\text{protein (g)}}{\text{required}} = \frac{40 \times \text{energy supplied/day}}{4.184}$$

So, in this example:

$$\text{protein g/day} = \frac{40 \times 137.2}{4.184} = 1312$$

5.6kg of hay (80g protein/kg) will supply:

$$5.6 \times 80 = 448g \text{ protein}$$

7.4kg of cereal (100g protein/kg) will supply:

$$7.4 \times 100 = 740g \text{ protein}$$

Thus, the total protein supplied will be (448 ÷ 740) = 1188g/day, equivalent to only 90 per cent of the horse's requirement. To meet the horse's need, it will be necessary to replace some of the cereal with soya which has a similar energy value to the cereal. If the forage supplied 448g protein, then the balance of the requirement (1312 – 448 = 864g) must be supplied in the hard feed which is fed 7.4kg in this example. We can determine the protein specification for the hard feed in the same way as we determined the energy specification. The concentration of protein required is 864 ÷ 7.4 = 117g/kg. Now we can use a Pearson's Square to proportion the cereal with soya to achieve the appropriate mix:

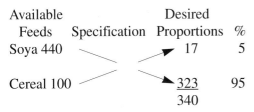

Available Feeds	Specification	Desired Proportions	%
Soya 440		17	5
Cereal 100		323	95
		340	

Thus, a mixture of cereal and soya that contains 58 per cent soya will contain 117g protein per kg. Since 7.4kg of hard feed are given daily then this must contain 370g of soya and the balance will be cereal. It is usual to mix up greater quantities at a time since it would be tedious to weigh out different quantities of soya for each horse. If the yard depended on the same feeds, hay and cereal, then all the horses would require supplementary protein and so it would be more practical to mix up 500kg at a time including 25kg soya, the balance (475kg) being cereal. The daily ration for the 500kg horse in full work would be 5.6kg hay, 7.03kg cereal and 0.37kg soya.

After protein, it would be necessary to check the supplies of both calcium and sodium and this can be done by drawing up a simple balance sheet (see Table 14.1)

It is clear that a simple ration such as this is severely deficient in major minerals. Calcium deficiency can be rectified by using limestone, an unpalatable rock (the quantity required depending on the source of limestone whose calcium content can vary between 33 and 38 per cent). If we assume a limestone with a calcium content of 33 per cent (330g/kg) then we can calculate how much to add as follows:

Table 14.1 Calcium and sodium balance

Feeds	Calcium supplied (g)	Sodium supplied (g)
5.6kg hay	17	10
7.03kg cereal	5	1.5
0.37kg soya	1	–
Totals	23	11.5
Requirements (g)	40	40
Deficits (g)	17	28.5

$$\text{limestone required (g)} = \frac{\text{calcium deficit}}{330} \times 1000$$

$$= \frac{17}{330} \times 1000 = 51.5g$$

It would be necessary to add this **daily** to the ration, split over the different feeds which should be top-dressed with any additives. Sodium deficiencies can be rectified by adding salt which contains about 40 per cent (400g/kg) sodium. The calculation is as follows:

$$\text{salt required (g)} = \frac{\text{sodium deficit}}{400} \times 1000$$

$$= \frac{28.5}{400} \times 1000 = 71.3g$$

Again this should be split over the feeds and top-dressed. Apart from these major deficiencies, there may be trace element and vitamin shortages which are best made good by using a good quality, general purpose supplement containing plenty of vitamin E.

An alternative to using limestone, which is unpalatable, to make good calcium deficiencies is to use organic sources of calcium. One such source is dehydrated lucerne which may contain about 18g of calcium per kg fed and can replace some of the hay in the ration. Replacement of 1kg of hay in the above ration with dried lucerne would give a **net** gain of 15g of calcium which nearly makes good the deficit of 17g. A replacement with 1.3kg lucerne for 1.3 kg hay would not only rectify the calcium deficiency but also lead to a net gain of 91g of protein because lucerne usually contains a minimum of 15 per cent protein (150g/kg) compared to the hay, which only contains 8

per cent (80g/kg) in this example. The original, calculated protein deficit was 124g, so the use of a little more lucerne in place of this hay would remove both the protein and the calcium deficits.

It will be apparent that juggling around with all these figures is quite time consuming and also rather difficult if you do not have all of the figures to hand. Fortunately there is now a computer programme available, called FeedCheck, which I have developed to take care of all of these difficulties. It contains a database of feeds which can be updated by the user, as well as a means of calculating your horse's needs. The programme compares what you are feeding with the horse's requirement and you can see at a glance if the diet is adequate. In many cases, you will find that you are overfeeding supplements and that, by their removal from the ration, you will be able to make significant savings. It also allows you to try using other feeds in the ration and see what effect they have on the overall nutrient supply. With a little bit of trial and error you will be able to simplify the horse's diet with the certain knowledge that he is getting what he needs rather than what some salesman would have you believe he should have.

If you use simple combinations of roughage and commercially compounded feed then, in most cases, the ration will contain all the nutrients required. The only likely exception is with horses that work hard at high ambient temperatures when they may sweat a lot. If this is the case, electrolytes may need to be added to the feed, in particular sodium (*see* Chapter 12). Normally compounded diets would not contain enough sodium for these extreme situations.

Table 14.2 Composition of common horse feeds (values expressed on as-fed basis)

Feed type	Digestible energy MJ/kg	Protein g/kg	Fibre g/kg	Calcium g/kg	Phosphorus g/kg	Sodium g/kg
Barley	12.8	95	50	0.6	3.3	0.1
Extruded barley	13.5	100	45	0.7	4.0	–
Micronized barley	14.0	99	50	0.4	2.4	–
Oats	11.2	99	100	0.7	3.0	0.1
Naked oats	13.6	112	25	0.6	3.5	0.2
Maize	14.2	86	25	0.2	3.0	0.1
Full fat soya	16.2	355	50	2.4	5.3	0.1
Soya 44	13.3	440	62	2.4	6.3	1.0
Soya oil	35.0	–	–	–	–	–
Wheat bran	10.8	132	110	2.1	8.5	–
Sugar beat pulp	9.0	98	170	7.1	0.7	–
Barley straw	6.0	34	380	3.8	0.6	0.9
Oat straw	6.5	44	390	3.4	0.6	1.0
Chaff	7.9	40	260	–	–	–
Alfalfa (dehy)	9.0	150	230	18.0	2.0	1.2
Grass (dehy)	12.5	160	220	6.0	3.0	2.0
Grass: poor	2.0	16	62	0.8	0.5	0.2
average	2.4	30	54	1.0	0.4	0.3
good	2.8	40	36	1.4	0.56	0.6
Hay: poor	7.0	45	360	2.0	1.2	0.8
average	8.0	70	300	5.0	2.5	2.0
good	9.5	100	270	6.3	3.1	2.2
Haylage	3.5	44	109	1.6	1.0	1.6
Bagged grass	4.5	45	165	2.5	1.5	2.2
Horse & pony cube	9.0	105	140	15.0	7.0	3.2
High fibre cube	8.5	100	200	10.0	5.0	3.2
Racing mix	13.5	140	60	12.0	6.0	5.0
Limestone	–	–	–	340	–	–
Dicalcium PO$_4$	–	–	–	240	185	–
Monocalcium PO$_4$	–	–	–	160	240	–
Salt	–	–	–	–	–	400

E<small>NERGY FOR</small> P<small>REGNANCY</small> <small>AND</small> L<small>ACTATION</small>

Pregnancy has little effect on energy requirements and mares are fed as though they are at maintenance (unless in work) up to the ninth month of pregnancy. During the ninth, tenth and eleventh months energy intake is increased by 1.11, 1.13 and 1.20 times maintenance respectively.

Other nutrients are balanced in the ration as shown previously. During lactation, for the first three months, energy requirements are increased to about 1.7 times maintenance and after this period, energy needs decline to about 1.5 times maintenance. A common problem in studs is the failure to adjust the protein level of the stud mix to suit the roughage fed. It is not uncommon in the early stages of lactation for mares to be fed a 50:50 mix of forage and concentrate. Mares need 12 per cent protein overall in the ration and thus, if the forage contains 8 per cent, protein, the forage proportion will only contribute 4 per cent protein (8 × 50/100) to the overall ration. This means the concentrate has to make up the balance of 8 per cent which means that the concentrate must contain 16 per cent (8 × 100/50) as a minimum. It is fairly common for stud cubes/mixes to contain 16 per cent protein but the problem arises when the forage contains less than 8 per cent. For example, a 6 per cent protein forage contributes 3 per cent (6 × 50/100) to the final mix leaving the concentrate to contribute 9 per cent, which means that it must contain a minimum of 18 per cent (9 × 100/50) protein. The situation is worsened if the concentrate makes up less than 50 per cent of the ration since it will have to contain more protein to make up the deficit. For example a 75 per cent forage (7 per cent protein) to 25 per cent concentrate will require that the concentrate contains 27 per cent protein (!) to achieve 12 per cent across the ration. It is no surprise to learn that mares fed entirely on dry feed are often fed insufficient protein. So, whilst as a general rule, the use of compound will remove the risk of nutrient deficiency it is always worth checking the protein content of the accompanying forage. Reliance on indifferent grass hays can result in underfeeding protein.

Summary Points
- Carefully determine the weight of the animal.
- Determine maintenance energy requirements.
- Adjust energy requirements according to the physiological need of the individual horse.
- Select feed ingredients of known energy value.
- Use only good quality forage.
- Estimate appetite and determine the minimum dietary energy concentration required.
- Proportion feeds on an energy basis, then check protein and major mineral supplies – balance as necessary.
- Confirm adequacy of ration by regularly reweighing, noting condition.

INDEX

absorption (of nutrients), sites of
29–30
acid, ascorbic 52
lactic 22, 23
neutralization of 20
pangamic 55
pantothenic 55
See also amino acids, fatty acids
acidity 40
additives 94
alfa A 85
alfalfa 85, 86
pellets 85
alkalinity 40
amino acids 37, 38, 94
anions 123–4
azoturia, 141, 144

bark eating 16
barley 87–8
behaviour, abnormal 18
browsing, 16
feeding, 14, 18
normal, 14
bile 23
bioflavanoids 56
biotin 55
blood: clotting mechanisms 52
coagulation of 41
body: fat stores 133
fluid regulation 42
bone malformation 40
bran 88
broodmare, nutrition of 109–11

caecum 24, 30
calcium 29, 40, 41, 122
deficiency 42
calories 31
carbohydrate 27, 31
metabolism of 42
overloading of 62
cardiac sphincter 21
carnitine 55
carotene 48
cations 124–5
cellulose 25
breakdown of 24
plant 25
cereals 86–7

chaff 84–5
herb 84
chewing, act of 20
rates 21
chloride 30, 40, 123
chlorine 44
choline 55
coarse mixes 93
cobalamin 54
cobalt 46, 2
cod-liver oil 48, 50
colic 24, 27, 146–7
gas 147
impaction 147
sand 17, 147
colon 24, 29, 30
compound feed 90–2
labelling of 90–2
types of 92–3
condition scoring 151–2
concentrates 18
energy 86–8
feeding of 106–7
protein 88–9
quantity 107
COPD 102
copper, 41, 46
poisoning 41
creep-feeding 114
crib-biting 18, 140
cubes 93

dental features 10
diet: balanced 40
straw-based 104
digestive: development 7
disorders 134–48
system 8
digestion 38
balance of 26
duration of 27
domestication, consequences of
57–60
duodenum 22, 23
dust-mites 101

electrolytes 30, 123–4
in sweat 126–7
supplements 127
energy 31, 122
environmental effects on 99
for maintenance 148–53
for pregnancy and lactation 158

for work 153–6
metabolism of 41, 130
sources of 36, 130–1
enzymes 25, 29
activity of 41
epiphysitis 43
exhaustion 34
extruded products 23, 93

fat: body stores 133
digestion of 23
fatty acids 29
volatile 27, 30, 36–7
feed: values 158
feeding, recommendations 132
strategies 131
systems 148
fencing 64
fermentation, caecal 9, 13
hind gut 7
process of 7
fibre, dietary 28
fish-meal 39, 44
white 89
fluorine 41
foal, artificial rearing of 117
neonate 45
practical feeding of 117
growth 113, 115
nutrition of 112
folacin 55
food: intake 141–2
processing 20
selection of 19
utilization of 9, 17
forage 100–6

gas removal 24
gastric juice 22
glucose 9, 29, 32, 36, 88, 133
absorbed 39
blood levels of 34
metabolism of 23
glycerol 29
glycogen reserves 33
grass 59–62, 65–73
bagged 83, 104
conserved 75–6
dried 81
growth 62–3, 77
hydroponic 81–3
leys 62
liveries 64

INDEX

quality of 65–9
  silage 83
grazing, 57–73
  species 62–3

haemoglobin 44
hay 77–80
  alternatives for 80–6, 103
  baling of 101
  barn-dried 80
  mouldy 100–2
  selection of 79–80
haylage 83
heat: increment 130
  load 129
  production 131
herbale 84
herbs 59–60, 70, 94
Hi-Fi 85
high fibre: diet 7
  foods 32
hot climates, feeding in 127–9
Hygrass 83

ileum 23
inappetance 133
insulin 34
iodine 31, 46
iron 44, 123

jejunum 23

keratin 55

lactation 113
laminitis 23–4, 27, 39, 144–6
  causes of 144
  diet for 145–6

large intestine 23, 24, 29
lawns 57
legumes 59
linseed 88–9
lysine 39

magnesium 42
maize 88
manganese 45
metabolic disease 28
microbial degradation 27
micronized products 23
micronutrients 70–1
micro-organisms 24, 25–7, 28, 29,

38, 73, 97
milk composition 112
Miller's disease 42
mineral imbalances 40, 142–4
minerals, major 40–4, 71
  trace 44–7, 71, 72, 94, 122
mould, effects of 102
myoglobin 44

niacin 54
nutrients 29, 76
  source of 131
  values of 98, 103

oats 87
oesophagus 21
oil 88
old age 134
overgrazing 69
overweight 137–8

pancreas 23
pancreatic juice 23
parasites 135
pasture, see grazing
peas and beans 89
performance, feeding for 121–7,
  132–3
phosphorus 30, 40, 41–2, 122
poaching, land 69
poisonous plants 58
potassium 30, 40, 42–3, 123
probiotics 94, 96–7
protein 94, 121
proteins 37
  animal 38
  plant 37
  soya 38
pyridoxine 54

quidding 19

rectum 24
riboflavin 53
roughage 18, 74–86
  alfalfa-based 85
  comparisons 86
  straw-based 84
roughs 57

saliva 20
selenium 41, 46
small intestine 23, 29

sodium 30, 40, 43, 73, 123
  chloride 43
  deficiency 43
soya 39
  bean 89
stable vices 139–41
stabling 17, 138–9
stallion, nutrition of 111–12
starch 23
stomach 21, 22, 29
straw 84, 105
sugars, simple 32
sulphur 44
supplements 94–6
  choosing 95
  oversupply of 95
sweating 125–7
symbiotic microflora 28

teeth 10, 28
  incisors 10, 12, 19
  molar teeth 9, 10, 19
  role of 19
  wolf 10
temperature 133
thiamin 53
time budgets 15, 17
trickle feeders 57, 73
toxicosis 49
toxic goitre 46
tying up syndrome 47

underweight 135–7

visual processes 49
vitamin: A 48, 122
  B group 53
  C 52
  D 50, 122
  E 51, 123
  K 52, 122
vitamin-like substances 55–7
vitamins 40, 48–56, 94
  fat-soluble 48–52
  water-soluble 52–5, 123

water 30
  and electrolyte balance 125–6
weaning 114
weaving 18

zinc 45